WAKING UP

AN ALIVE JESUS CHANGES EVERYTHING

ZACK QUILICI

Book Formatting by Derek Murphy @Creativindie

WAKING UP
Copyright © 2019 by ZACK QUILICI.

For information contact :
http://www.ZACKQUILICI.com

Book and Cover design by ZACK QUILICI
ISBN 13 : 9781724472199

First Edition: JANURARY 2019

DEDICATION

Bryan Muche, That hallway changed my entire life.
Thank you for showing me Gods unconditional love.
Bounce house ministry baby.

THANK YOU

To everyone, who took the time to write something to be added to this book, writing this without your stories would be impossible, so THANK YOU for being courageous enough to let me add your life to my book.
To Jenny and Rob Morace, for taking the time to help me with this incredibly hard process. Your hearts are amazing! Rob thank you so much for the subtitle to this book, LOVE working with you!
Anne Parizeau, for all your hard work and doing it out of love, you're the reason this book is somewhat decent.
Holli Wright, you da bomb girl!
Maggie Nichols, your creative mind has been such a blessing to be around, thank you!

HEY

Prologue

DEPRESSED. Eyes are burning with guilt and exhaustion. I'm pulling up, parking near the entrance of this gym that I couldn't care less about. I sucked, the world sucked, being heartbroken sucked. It was another cold morning in the middle of November, but not cold enough to make the birds stop chirping. I love birds. I often say to myself "thirty seconds," and then sit there listening, not doing anything else but listening to the birds. Or sometimes it's the stars, maybe rain, or even a sunset. That thirty seconds could change my mood or day in an instant; it was a reminder that I wasn't too good for the little things in life.

"Why am I even here?"
"Gosh, my head hurts."

It's only been a week since getting dumped, but it's been an eventful one. I didn't care the day it happened, but man it's the only thing I can think of now- the girl, tripled with whiskey and weed. Reeking of alcohol, I walk up the four steps leading to the front door of the gym, opening it, and also opening the floodgates of emotions. Building this gym with my bare hands, but also building it with her, was making the wound even deeper. And I'm absolutely positive that being hungover didn't help.

"She's gone."
"You're such an idiot."

I closed the door, which was particularly great at letting anybody in the building know that someone had come in because of its squeak and antiquity. I miss that old, clangy warehouse door. One of my coaches, Justin, had gotten there before me, ready to coach the 9:30 a.m. group fitness class. Walking into the office, Justin was pumped up and ready to rumble, but he also knew what was going on. Not only an employee of mine, he was also my best friend. We worked out together, laughed, grew, and he ultimately did the most amazing thing a person could ever do; he never gave up on me.

"She's missing out."
"She won't find anyone better."

I was so consumed by this pain, confused by the erupting chaos of this situation that I was probably the most selfish I've ever been. The irrational thinking and the irrational drinking was unbelievable. I walked into the office, sat down on the couch, and stared at the wall. Staring at this beautiful logo of my gym, cut out of metal by a friend. It was the kind of stare that could last a lifetime, the one where it's impossible to blink. It had a simplistic effect that my whole life seemed to flash before me. The feeling of shock was sickening. Dazed, drunk, and confused. Justin interrupted, in what felt like perfect timing.

"How you doing, man?"

"Not good."

"How come?"

"She's gone, man. Like I don't know what to do."

"I'm so sorry…. Is there anything I can do to help fix this?"

"No, I just need her back. That would fix everything, everything will go back to normal. I'm sick of this pain. I'm sick of this."

"Okay… please let me know if I can help in any way."

"Can you coach the next class?"

"Yeah of course, man. And Zack... can I do something else for you?

"Yeah, man. What is it?"

"Can I pray for you?"

"Ha! Of course, pray for me, sure...."

In the moment, it was laughable. As I'm sitting here sulking in a heartbreak, here comes a right hook of grace to my soul. Justin was a very authentic man, with immense character, and I trusted him. He saw my flaws, my lifestyle, and worked for me for three years, knowing my lifestyle was not what God wanted for me. I was so oblivious to the situation and to what was about to happen next. He got up, sat right next to me. I thought it was going to be a hug and "I love you bro," but what happened next was the thing that shifted my entire life, my entire perspective, and opened my heart. He put his hand on my shoulder and *actually* prayed for me, right there. He talked to God like he talked to a friend. Simple, yet unrelentingly effective.

"God, I lift Zack up to you....
He's in pain.....
He needs comfort...
I know he doesn't seem to feel love from any direction...
I just want him to know that You love him...
Open his heart to you....

9

Amen."

I wasn't laughing about praying to a God that I didn't believe in anymore. It felt real, the love felt real, the connection felt real. But even though it was a moment of waking up, it didn't take the pain away. It didn't stop my bad habits going forward. Something was just different. I had a glimpse of hope for a solution. Anything to take this pain away. For the *first* time in my entire life... as I gazed again at the logo on the wall... the thought lingered... I wanted to go to church. God wasn't knocking anymore; He was opening the door.

"Maybe... just maybe... this is the solution."

✝

This weekend is the start of something new, something fresh, something exciting, something I've never done before, but I've always been good at this kind of thing. As I get out of my car, I always make sure that there isn't anything in my teeth from last night's 4 a.m. drunken fast-food meal. I make sure I don't have any bed head so it doesn't look like I just woke up, even though I just did.

And I always have some gum so my breath wouldn't smell like Jack Daniels whiskey from the night before.

"Gosh my head hurts."
"Am I still drunk?"

Today is first day that I am the front door greeter at church! It was so easy to be the first smiling face someone sees when they get to church and the last face when they leave. I love meeting new people and making them feel welcome, and I think having a bit of alcohol still in my system made it easy to be social. I'm full of excitement and energy, but unfortunately I have a huge heart of conviction as well. I always felt so much disappointment in myself during church; I found myself crying all the dang time because I knew what I was doing beforehand was the complete opposite of what God wanted for me. Drinking, cocaine, one night stands... I don't remember one night during this first month of going to church when I didn't load a bong full of marijuana. It was all great until I sat in that seat during church, regret, disappointment, and tears just *flooded*. I bet I could have filled up the baptism tank with all the water. I just didn't get it yet. UGH. I knew what I was doing wasn't helping at all; It was making me more depressed. My heart was still broken, and I don't know why I kept doing it.

†

It took some major decision-making when I resolved to leave my hometown and move to sunny San Diego. But now, the gym I used to own had been sold, and I was no longer willing or even able to participate in running the gym. I'm guessing a whole lot of ego and pride was involved. Half the time I was either hung-over or crying when I showed up to the gym, so it was probably a good thing that I left. I needed a fresh start, I needed to get away. Looking back, it was one of the best decisions I have ever made in my entire life. It may not be the answer for everyone, but it worked for me. You learn a whole bunch about yourself when you rely on nothing but God. So with three hundred bucks, my mattress, and a basket full of clothes, I loaded up my truck, and off I went.

†

I had been been in San Diego for about a month and it *still* hadn't clicked. I was still drinking and making a lot of bad decisions, and nothing changed until my brother Aaron….

Yep...had to do it. Had to take a break from the story and give a huge shout out to my twin brother Aaron, with the endless support, both financially and emotionally. He is known in my heart as the hardest working person I've ever met. And I know this is very cliché, especially to put it in a book... but man, I'm proud of you. I still can't believe we are twins, even more so than all the people we meet that make us have to pull out our IDs to prove we are twins. Sometimes still, I feel adopted because of how pretty you are. Like I said from day one, you should be a model and little do you know... there's still time to fulfill my dream for you. Ha! I love you, and I can't wait to do the rest of our lives together, and you're probably still and forever able to back squat more than me.

...came and paid me a visit, and we went to go see a San Diego Padres game. With excitement and the ability to really cover up what was really going on in my heart, I decided to get blackout drunk. I drank so much that when I woke up the next day, I realized that I didn't even remember any of the baseball game! I don't even remember embarrassing my brother. And I just was so fed up with it, I was so fed up with myself. And it was then that I did what everybody does at some point in their life, and I really looked myself in the mirror. That's when I saw him. I saw the man that was unbelievably broken, undeniably alone, and flat out lost. But I was okay with seeing that in my reflection, because it was about time that I came to that conclusion. It had been a long time coming.

"Dude… it's time. It's time to stop avoiding Jesus."

†

No one in the world likes their turkey cold. I know... You probably just got super mad and said "What? I DO!" Well, you can totally keep your cold turkey sandwiches... Let's just say I like warm turkey better, fresh from the oven on Thanksgiving, piled right on top of a mountain of mashed potatoes and then *BOOM,* a gallon of gravy over all of it. But I'm not talking about that. I'm talking about how I decided on that day- July 16, 2016- that I would stop drinking alcohol and quit *cold turkey*.

I wanted to live for something bigger than myself, and I knew, even then, that God had something insanely better for me than waking up hungover, driving drunk (who knows how many times), and embarrassing people. I figured out that my personality, which can obviously be taken as loud and obnoxious, is literally the same without alcohol. But with alcohol, I didn't know where to draw the line. I'd always cross it and drink too much. In my last book, I had some stories where I just kept punching people. So if I didn't know where that line was, I just decided to get rid of drinking, period. And it opened my eyes to so many things. I figured out how to have fun without it, to laugh without it, to be Zack, without it. You'd think someone would eventually learn how to stop hurting people and making mistakes, but that obviously doesn't just happen out of nowhere. I needed help, needed help knowing how to be a real man, how to control myself, learn my limits, and ultimately learn the lessons that would lead me to true happiness. And after I woke up, I learned that help can only come from one place- one unshakable and unrelenting place. Place? That's the wrong word. It's a person. You find that help in a person, and that person is Jesus Christ.

JESUS

INTRODUCTION

*I believe in Christianity as I believe that the sun has risen:
not only because I see it, but because by it I see
everything else.*

-C.S. Lewis

*I constantly wake up every morning trying to get better,
trying to improve, trying to walk closer to God*

-Tim Tebow

WHEN WE THINK of waking up, we instantly go toward the thought of physically waking up. Waking up to that annoying sound of your alarm, always wishing and hoping for ten more minutes. Completely understanding that ten more minutes won't do a dang thing to our day, but for some reason, you are the most comfortable you've ever been. The temperature is perfect and the position of your body and pillow is perfect, making falling asleep for ten more minutes easy, only to wake up ten minutes later and being insanely more exhausted. Waking up is difficult regardless who you are. I wonder if it was difficult for Adam to wake up when God created him. I can only imagine what his voice was like, roaring through Adam's ears and waking every part of his being, his heart starting to twitch, the sound of blood pumping through his veins like a thunderstorm. Imagination at its finest explodes when I think about the FIRST human being waking up for the FIRST time. Did he wake up scared? Was he

THE FIRST HUMAN BEING WAKING UP FOR THE FIRST TIME

dreaming before God woke him up? Did he wake up with a puffy face and blurry, booger-filled eyes? I don't wear contact lenses but waking up without the full capability of seeing scares me. I think that's what most of us figuratively walk around life with. A blurry perspective about God. A perspective that is clouded by your own wants, selfish desires, pride, skepticism and the need of a new set of contacts without even knowing it. Then all of a sudden it happens, you get that new set of contact lenses, that word perspective is clear, your eyes are open, the world is beautiful and what Jesus did for you on that cross is unmistakably something that you can't bypass anymore.

You can see. You can love, you can understand your purpose.

†

Sitting here in a taco shop in San Diego, California writing, I can't help to think about my perspective of God. Is it clear? Can I see and know him without anything getting in the way? How do I personally self reflect my perspective? Is it biblical? Often times we can get caught up in the thought of being "selfish" with our relationship with God. It's true, everybody's relationship is different. But is YOUR relationship healthy? This book is going to be filled with stories and truths that I personally had that ultimately made my perspective of God more clear. Things that I "woke up to" and said dang... now that makes sense. God's perspective is everything and it will change everything.

†

Since we are talking about perspective it makes me take a second look at things in the way God looks at them, getting Zack and his feelings out of the way is something that needs to be practiced and will never be perfected. But it has ultimately made me think, and honestly, thinking in the biblical sense was totally new. That's why the theme of this book is just to make you think.. Maybe you can relate to some of the stories, but maybe not. All my hope is for you to not get stuck… stuck in the sense of complacency.. waking up to things and what's going on in your life. Changing the way you think about God could honestly change your entire life. There are so many more things I'd like to write about with this theme, but for the sake of time, I did my best, so I kind of don't want to hear, "Zack, how could you not write about this…" Because I definitely probably thought of it, but regardless, I really do hope you enjoy this book. Before we get going… Thank you to those of you who supported my first book, *Be Brave.* It seriously means the world to me and joy is an understatement because honestly I'm still surprised it even happened. HA! But one of my favorite authors, Bob Goff, did something that was just amazing: he put his phone number in his book and if you had anything you wanted to talk to him about, you were able to. I went back and forth in my first book making the decision to not put my number in the book, but this time is different. I want you to know that I love you and I want to support you anyway I can, so here it is. 775-848-6169

LOVES

1

TO THE STRUGGLES

Each and everyday I wake up and thank God that one, I'm alive, and second that I'm not hung-over and covered in throw-up.

-Me

Consider how hard it is to change yourself, your habits and thoughts and then understand how much harder it is to change others. Leave it up to God, all you can do is show people Jesus. Focus on that.

-Me

DON'T ASK, I don't know why I decided to start this book off with the first chapter being about struggles. (I guess I just wanted to clear the air, getting rid of the dumb elephant in the room about the fact that some of you think since I work for a church and am a published author that I may have my life together.) The absolute and honest truth is, I don't and I don't think I ever will have my life together. I do believe people and I can be on the "right" track. I do believe the journey of sanctification and trying our best to be Christ-like is the right track, but man, oh man, does that come with some struggles!

†

In my last book *Be Brave*, I talk about a lot of the things that ultimately led me to Christ but it doesn't mean they went away. Almost three years later, there are some things that I struggle with unbelievably. Like my heartbreak is still real. I don't think of her all the time, constantly compare and wonder why she left me like I used to. But I do believe that I'm not completely over it. I'm way better than I used to be. But it still hurts and I'm not ashamed of saying that. My life is amazing and I don't complain a lot, but shoot, I'd be a liar to say I still don't miss her sometimes. But at the same time I can't help to remember a quote I heard,

"With heartbreak, expecting someone to get over it, is like telling an amputee that lost a limb to get over it, it will be forever a scar and a wound but it's definitely healed."

It's crazy, irrational and it doesn't make sense, it's just there. Does that remind you of anything? It reminds me of another love that doesn't make sense but it's real, and of course, that's the love of Jesus Christ to us. Without it, there's no way in the world I'd be where I'm at today. Without Jesus, that heartbreak would consume me like it did in the past, but as of right now, it's just a part of my story. It's the story of how I was so

WITH A HEARTBREAK, EXPECTING SOMEONE TO "GET OVER IT" IS LIKE TELLING AN AMPUTEE THAT LOST A LIMB TO "GET OVER IT"

broken that I was searching for a solution, crying every single day and wondering why I exist. It's easily the focal point of my testimony now and I can't seem to get past it. At the same time, I don't want to. It's the way I can connect with others, because I'm not the only one in this world that has gone through a heartbreak; I just now know a solution. In my opinion, if you can pinpoint a time or situation in your life that you can say to yourself "Yep, without God, I don't think I would've made it out of that time of my life alive. God saved me." If you can say that.. and honestly mean it.. I believe that story no longer belongs to you. That story belongs to God and his church. That story is the way you show others what Jesus did for you. It might sound harsh, but I believe it's true. You are being selfish when you keep that story to yourself.

My mouth still waters when I smell alcohol.. The aroma of it makes me think back of all the "good" times that I've had in the past. I'm more than two years sober as I'm writing this and I have no desire to go back, but I'd be a liar if I don't have those nights that I think about how cool it was to get off work, text the bros and get drunk. Life was easier back then. Ministry is hard, but it's understanding the mission I'm on that makes getting rid of those thoughts somewhat easy. It's understanding who I am in Christ that makes it easy. What I'm not saying is that alcohol is evil. I think it's great as long as you can control yourself; I had no self control. I can't help pointing out how I love the way the Apostle Peter writes about this.

Since Jesus went through everything you're going through and more, learn to think like him. Think of your sufferings as a weaning from that old sinful habit of always expecting to get your own way. Then you'll be able to live out your days free to pursue what God wants instead of being tyrannized by what you want.

You've already put in your time in that God-ignorant way of life, partying night after night, a drunken and profligate life. Now it's time to be done with it for good. Of course, your old friends don't understand why you don't join in with the old gang anymore. But you don't have to give an

account to them. They're the ones who will be called on the carpet—and before God himself.
1 Peter 4:1-5 MSG

In all honesty.. I don't think I could write about this and be open if I didn't FULLY understand who and what my identity is. I can grimace, get cold about my past life and have regret flood in, but man, I can see who I am. I can see clearly now that the rain is gone (ha). I can see myself, my past, and my mistakes the way God sees them. I wish I could sit here and say I never struggle with that stuff anymore, but its true... I struggle and I pray A LOT. I so desperately want this pain in my chest to leave. Knowing the truth, knowing who my savior is, while at the same time struggling with a lot of things is hard to swallow.

†

One of the biggest struggles that I'm dealing with right now is the relationship with my dad and I can't explain it. It's kind of at a standstill with our conversations and I hate it. He doesn't know me or what's going on in my life and I don't seem to know him or what's going on in his. He doesn't seem to care and neither do I. I love him to death and if it wasn't for him, I wouldn't be the man I am today. But I don't know what happened. I don't know why, but we're just so disconnected and it makes me sick to my stomach, and I miss him. I beat myself up all the time because the Bible is full of commands to respect and honor your father. This is what Ephesians says :

Children, do what your parents tell you. This is only right. "Honor your father and mother" is the first commandment that has a promise attached to it, namely, "so you will live well and have a long life." Fathers, don't exasperate your children by coming down hard on them. Take them by the hand and lead them in the way of the Master.

Ephesians 6:1-4 The Message (MSG)

†

Am I honoring my father? Am I obeying him? What does this verse have anything to do with my father if he's not a Christian?

†

Uhg.I just remind myself that God can do anything and can mend any broken relationship. I so desperately want to tell him how much it hurt my feelings when he visited me and didn't even want to visit the church I was working for. But as fast as those thoughts come into my heart, they make an even faster exit. I understand that I'm being selfish; I understand that all I want to talk about with my dad is Jesus. Not sports, not fishing, not anything other than Jesus. He has such an amazing story, personality and heart; Jesus would be stoked to have him on His team! He would help so many people. I often think of an imaginary scenario that he would quit his job right now and together we would open a church, make a huge impact and high five in heaven. I know his people skills, I know his heart, I know his personality and I know how much he would impact the world for the kingdom of Christ. I often fall under the category of "wanting things more than they do." I want his perspective to be shifted, I want his heart to be opened and I want to do life with him and pursue everything related to God.

> GOD NEVER PROMISES TO REMOVE US FROM OUR STRUGGLES. HE DOES PROMISE, HOWEVER, TO CHANGE THE WAY WE LOOK AT THEM – MAX LUCADO

†

Do I REALLY forgive him? What does the Bible say about forgiveness? What did he do that he needs forgiveness for?

Did I apologize for what I needed to apologize for? Did he?

†

I don't like the idea of having daddy issues but it definitely is the truth. I try to do everything on my own and I never reach out to him because I don't think I'll ever be at the point of making him proud. All I desire is his support and I love him so much. This is hard for me to write about.. But like I said, if you have any advice for me, that number in the introduction is my actual number and I would love any help if you've been through a similar situation. But let me remind you... Being a Christian when your dad is not, isn't easy and it upsets me. But I'll continue to pray and if you don't mind, pray for my pride because I also understand that reaching out to someone goes both ways.

YOU

2

TO THE SICK

We want to avoid suffering, death, sin and ashes. But we live in
a world crushed, broken and torn, a world God Himself visited
to redeem. We receive his poured-out life, and being allowed to
the high privilege of suffering with him, may we then pour
ourselves out for others.

- Elisabeth Elliot

I JUST KNEW, I knew that I had to send a
prayer out to our God, the King of Kings and the Lord of
Lords for strength. I've known myself to break down
during these moments, but I wanted to be strong, not for

me, but for him. I wanted the discernment and the right words to say, pray and speak. Walking out of that elevator, I have a very small understanding that we live in a broken world and it just sucks. Walking down the long quiet hallway, walking up to the front desk realizing that we are in the wrong section of the hospital because our friend isn't in the childbirth section. As we turn back towards the elevator, I think I thanked God for more time to think, more time to pray and more time to take some deep breaths.

†

Walking into that room, I saw a guy whom I remembered as a very fit, happy charismatic, joyful and loving. He was that type of guy who would bring life to any room he entered. He had that spark of energy that the class needed. You see, I had the opportunity to be one of the coaches that taught Mike how to be fit. He was one my clients in a group fitness class environment and he was always that guy who brought that energy that every coach loved. Working out isn't always easy, but he was a guy who understood that. He also understood that being around his closest friends and playing 80's music while working out made the hard work fun. That excitement is priceless and his smile and jokes were always a blessing to those around him.

†

But today I barely recognized him.. I knew it was Mike but there were tubes down his throat and his body was frail from losing weight. He wasn't able to get up, smile or give me one of those sweaty hugs that I was used to. He was sleeping and fighting really hard to stay alive. This brain cancer was tearing him apart; everything I knew about that guy was the complete opposite. After about a minute of looking at him and while I was looking out his window at the beautiful view of San Diego, he woke up. When he saw my friend Leslie and me, the machine to the left started to beep quite ferociously and I kind of freaked out a bit. But when the nurse rushed in, he told us he was just excited to see us. Realizing that he can see us and understand who we are told me that the Mike I knew was in there. He wasn't able to talk but when the doctor came in and performed some little motor skill exercises, again the realization of Mike being there was true. He could hear us. So he could hear a prayer too.

†

For the first time since following Christ and I'm sure It's not going to be the last, where I asked, "God, why couldn't you have picked somebody else?" As selfish, arrogant and stupid it is to wish this upon anybody else, it was my first reaction to the situation. I loved Mike. I know it's a broken world and I know that's not the way I'm supposed to think. But I was mad at God. It was calming to know that God didn't design the world this way and He didn't want this either. But honestly, it didn't help the frustration because I know that God can change anything He wants. As I prepared myself to pray for Mike, I remembered that he wasn't a Christian since the last time we spoke about it. But anything is possible and the timeframe of Mike's life was nearing the end. I wanted him to get a chance to hear about how God loves him, so I took the opportunity, knowing that I might've been the only person to pray for him and his salvation. (I could be wrong, but I wasn't going to miss this opportunity.) After praying for him, I looked him right in the eye and told him to squeeze my hand as hard as he can if he understood how much I loved him. Seeing his tears roll down his cheek was the most heartbreaking yet reassuring thing that has happened to me in a long time. He heard me, he heard my prayer and hopefully, he may have received Christ. I won't know for sure until I get to heaven.

And at that given moment I got sick, sick of thinking about how fallen the world is with diseases, with mental illnesses, with suicide and all the things that don't have a cure. Waking up to reality of how wrecked the world is broke my heart. Understanding that people lose their lives every day due to these things. Frustration at its finest is when I think of how many times Jesus healed people; the blind, lame, paralyzed, bleeding and from leprosy. I just wanted my friend to get healed. I just wanted Him to heal Mike, to give Mike his life back, so I can selfishly enjoy his presence. But God is all knowing and all powerful and his plans are not for me to understand.

So as I dealt with all that frustration, anger, and all the confusion about how the world is with all these diseases that people can't do anything about, it got me thinking. Thinking about something that we were all born with: a sinful nature. Something so wicked and rotten to its core with no

> FOR WE ALL HAVE
> SINNED AND FALLEN
> SHORT OF THE
> GLORY OF GOD
> ROMANS 3:23

hope for a cure except Jesus. It's hard to think about, but even when Jesus doesn't heal every disease or circumstance, He gives us a simple hope. Without that hope and without Him we would have to deal with all these diseases, sicknesses and losing loved ones alone. My goodness, without that hope, we have no future, we have no purpose, we have no security in knowing where our friends or loved ones are going. So as I am still waking up to the idea that the world is broken, I want to encourage you to please understand that when we get frustrated with the what this broken world throws at us, just remember that we have a hope and we have a future, *IF* we put that trust in Jesus Christ. I know it doesn't take the initial pain away and it could take a very long time to recover from a devastating loss, but when you can say "He/She is in God's hands" and REALLY believe it, you end up coming to a conclusion that God really does come through. Driving away from that hospital, I was able to get a grasp of my frustration and say to myself.. "God's got this." But to this day, I still hate cancer.

Below is a list of Jesus' healings in the Gospels, all 26 of them.

1. The Nobleman's Son (John 4:46).
2. The Man with an Unclean Spirit (Mark 1:21, Luke 4:31).
3. Simon Peter's Mother-in-Law (Matt 8:14, Mark 1:29, Luke 4:38).
4. The Healing of the Leper (Matthew 8:1, Mark 1:40, Luke 5:12).
5. The Healing of the Paralytic (Matthew 9:1, Mark 2:1, Luke 5:17).
6. The Man at Bethesda pool (John. 5:2).
7. The Man with the Withered Hand (Matthew 12:9, Mark 3:1, Luke 6:6).
8. The Centurion's Servant (Matthew 8:5; Luke 7:2)
9. Widow's Deceased Son (Luke 7:11)
10. Demoniacs at Gadara (Matthew 8:28; Mark 5:1; Luke 8:26)
11. Woman with the Issue of Blood (Matthew 9:20; Mark 5:25; Luke 8:43)

12. Jairus's Deceased Daughter (Matthew 9:18; Mark 5:21; Luke 8:40)
13. Two Blind Men (Matthew 9:27)
14. Mute, Possessed Man (Matthew 9:32)
15. Daughter of Canaanite (Matthew 15:21; Mark 4:24)
16. Deaf Man with Impediment (Mark 7:32)
17. Blind Man at Bethsaida (Mark 8:22)
18. Epileptic Boy (Matthew 17:14; Mark 9:14; Luke 9:37)
19. Man Born Blind (John 9:1)
20. Man, Blind, Dumb, Possessed (Matthew 12:22; Luke 11:14)
21. Woman Bent Double (Luke 13:10)
22. Man with Dropsy (Luke 14:1)
23. Lazarus (John 11:11)
24. Ten Lepers (Luke 17:11)
25. Blind Bartimaeus (Matt 20:29; Mark 10:45; Luke 18:35)
26. Malchus (Luke 22:50)

INCREDIBLY

3

TO THE FEAR

God actually commands us not to fear, or worry. The phrase
"fear not" is used at least 80 times in the Bible, most likely
because He knows the enemy uses fear to decrease our hope
and limit our victories. I've been a Christian for 15 years now,
and I'm still in awe that God, who created the universe, cares
about every detail of our lives. We belong to an all-powerful, all-
knowing, victorious father who cares deeply about us. When we
really meditate on this truth, it's hard to remain fearful about the
trials we face. By focusing on Him, and how He considers us his
prized, redeemed ones, our focus naturally shifts from fear to
faith. Jesus himself expressed fear to the point of sweating blood,
so God understands fear is natural. But whatever you're fearing-
a health crisis, family problem, financial struggle- focus on the
power of a God who calls you by name, and commands fear to
flee from you heart.
-Jessica Kastner

I CAN ONLY imagine, heck I don't think I can
give myself enough credit to even imagine something like
that. Here people are, innocent people, enjoying
themselves with not a care in the world. Sipping on their
beer and grooving to the best music in the world. Country
music. Yes, I said it. Paying a lot of money to see the best
country music artists in the world, I bet people were pretty
ticked off when one of them just decided out of nowhere

to run offstage and not sing anymore in the middle of his set. Confusion, frustration and just flat out anger began to boil in these loyal fans. CRACK. CRACK. CRACK.

"At first we didn't believe it was gunfire but when I saw the singer go off stage, I looked at my girlfriend and said, "Run!".

"She laughed, thinking I was over-reacting. People around us were still dancing.

"I ran to a fence backstage. People started going through barbed wire. One friend kicked it down.

"A girl next to us got shot. A guy next to us got shot.

"I called my Mum that night. There are about 10 minutes that I can't remember anymore. She said I told her there were bodies everywhere. But I don't remember seeing any of that.

"For the first two days I drank. I didn't want to deal with it. I kept hearing gunshots and having flashbacks.

"I went to a concert three days later and I realised that going out and talking to people who were also at Route 91 that night was therapeutic.

"That's how talking about that night makes me feel - each time, it feels less raw.

"It was a horrific experience, but in an odd way, I'm thankful to experience the after-effects. You see the best of humanity after a disaster.

"My lowest moment was last weekend - I went to a memorial for one of the victims, it's just so sad to see the families of these people who died.

"Since the shootings, I've become a better listener and certainly more compassionate... I've never hugged more grown men in my life than in the past month.

"The conspiracy theories don't make me angry - I certainly don't know all the facts. But it certainly wasn't fake.

"I'm impressed with how many people are willing to go back out to concerts. The country scene is a tight community.

"One psycho can't dictate how a bunch of people live their lives." (1)

Jason Aldean is one of my favorite country music artists. With a few of his songs memorized enough to play them on my guitar, I was a fan and I was proud of it. Country concerts are always the best time; the songs are always talking about American pastimes. Heartbreaks, dogs and fishing are what most songs are about and heck, do I love all three of those! They might as well be my middle name. But let's get real, I never thought

STEPHEN PADDOCK

that a man who obviously didn't know that Jesus loved him would open fire at the concert I was at. His name is Stephen Paddock and he lost the battle and the war when he open fired with multiple assault rifles from a room overlooking the concert in the Mandalay Bay, killing 59 people and injuring almost 600 more. This isn't going to be a detailed report of what happened on that horrible night. So if this is your first time hearing about this tragedy, google it and get intertwined with what went down.

The one word I want us to focus on, especially if you call yourself a Christian and trust Jesus with your whole life, is FEAR. In the Bible its states many times that the word fear should easily be succumbed by the grace of God. As it says in the first chapter in the book of Joshua verse one of the Old Testament.

"Have I not commanded you? Be strong and courageous. Do not be terrified; do not be discouraged, for the Lord your God will be with you wherever you go." Joshua 1:9

The context of this verse is when Moses died and Joshua was anointed to be the next leader of the Israel nation. The LORD came to Joshua and gave him hope and encouraged him that no matter where he goes, or what he does, the LORD will be with him. So fear was not an option. If you have God on your side then fear might as well be erased from your dictionary. The reason I bring this up is because the conversation of fear happened at our Bible study growth group following the Vegas shooting. Many members of the group were stating things like,

"Now I'm scared to go to concerts."
"Big crowds scare me anyways."
"I'm definitely thinking twice about big events."

Now as the leader of the growth group, I had to step in and make everyone understand that yes, this was a huge horrific tragedy, but we cannot and will not let the devil win this one, making us think twice about the comfort we received through our salvation. First, we need to do something simple. In Romans chapter 12:15 the apostle Paul wrote, "Rejoice with those who rejoice; mourn with those who mourn." So be there for the people that are affected emotionally, be the presence that gives comfort first. Then we need to be able to go to any event and big crowd with our chins held high, knowing that the Savior of the world is on our side. We aren't afraid of death; death was defeated on the cross. Death should not be something that ignites fear inside of us. We, as Christians, know where we are going and how happy it makes us to think about it. Heaven awaits us no matter how we die.

> WE AREN'T AFRAID OF DEATH, DEATH WAS DEFEATED WITH THE CROSS

Now the sad and ultimate truth is that when I was reading through every single victim's online obituary, there was only ONE person that was known for their love of Christ. Now I know I didn't personally know anybody. I just read what the reports said. I've always been optimistic so the thought of there being more Christians that died during the event is very appealing since I didn't get that much info on the victims. This paragraph isn't easy to write, but it's the truth and sometimes the truth hurts. Did all those victims that were not known for their love for Christ go to hell? Even if they were innocent and got brutally murdered? Did God protect the majority of Christians during the massacre? It makes my stomach ache and wanting to puke is on the forefront of my mind, thinking about how all those innocent lives got taken. But that brings up a VERY important couple of questions, doesn't it? Are you scared to die? What are you going to be known for if you die?

I don't know about you, but as a Christian man who is a fully devoted follower of Jesus Christ, I know I'm not scared to die. I want my online obituary to say that I followed Jesus and I want my life to reflect that and I want it to reflect it HARD. We never know when or how we are going to die, but we can know where we are going. So that word fear should be an eye-opener to you. The Vegas shooting should be an eye opener for everyone, knowing that you can die having fun at a concert. So if the word fear is bringing up bad and anxious feelings, you might have to reexamine your relationship with your Lord and Savior or you just might have to take that Bible off your shelf and dust it off.

†

Going into another story about fear.. I just had to let one of my brothers in Christ tell this story. Mr. Billy Graham himself. I didn't get the chance to meet him, but you bet I'll be excited to meet him in heaven. What a man of God he was. This was from his book "The Reason for my Hope."

†

Do you think He's coming back? People flocked to the most highly anticipated Hollywood movie release in the summer of 2012 for the answer.

Who were they talking about? The legendary comic-strip superhero of the 1940's, a caped crusader who triumphs over arch villains. Batman had been idolized in print, television, and more recently in theaters. As a boy, I loved comic books and read every one I could get my hands on, more than once. The stories I read taught the lesson that evil deeds will be trampled and victory will reign. What was once a form of comic entertainment for children has become a cosmic adventure for adults who find delight in a new pop-culture phenomenon: the emergence of recreational evil. Many see it as frivolous until it's reality fills hearts with trepidation.

"THE REASON
FOR MY HOPE"
BILLY GRAHAM
PAGES 155-157

On July 20, 2012, fans filled movie theaters for the premier of Warner Brothers' production The Dark Knight Rises in which citizens of the fictitious Gotham City wonder if Batman will come back to save their cosmopolitan way of life from nuclear annihilation.

While the plot is fictional, it profiles humanity's great search to understand good and evil. But an astonishing story emerged when the evil characters, not the hero, seemed to capture the admiration of fans. Many arrived in costumes to mimic the villains.

The Telegraph in London wrote that the movie was a "superhero film without a superhero" because the would-be superstar faltered in many ways and illustrious criminals had a greater allure to wild imaginations. One reviewer noted that Bane, the primary villain, "wears a ventilator mask and fills the morgue with innocents" and another claimed the Tom Hardy character "was able to execute emotion and intimidate the audience using just his eyes and forehead." The film's director, Christopher Nolan, added in an interview that the character is "very complex and very interesting and…. People will be very entertained by him." Newsweek simply reported that, "Audiences will be blown away."

So electrifying was the marketing campaign that people around the world stood in lines at 6:30 in the morning to buy advance tickets while others avoided queues by going online to purchase the right to occupy the coveted seats.

The multimillion-dollar advertising campaign thrilled fans with anticipation worldwide, from Australia to Korea to France. Lavish trailers designed to tantalize the emotions and lure entertainment seekers revealed morsels of the plot's prophecy. "A fire will rise" splashed across the screen, throngs of people were eerily chanting, and a scene where Catwoman whispers to Batman's alter ego, "There's a storm coming, Mr. Wayne."

In spite of a caution that children ages thirteen and under should not see the movie, fans brought children as young as five years old and filled an Aurora, Colorado, theater, ecstatic to attend the midnight premiere of the predicted blockbuster film.

While the audience was captivated by the high-tech drama and powerful violence, a twenty-four-year-old man slipped into the theater wearing a gas mask and tactical gear. Moviegoers who noticed him thought he as part of a publicity stunt to promote the film. Instead, a premeditated attack began with tear gas followed by dispersing ammunition into the audience of eyewitnesses. Within minutes chaos turned into carnage, and the theater became a sinister crime scene.

When the raid ceased, the perpetrator disappeared from the theater. When captured, he introduced himself as the Joker. He certainly had not entertained a crowd as the villains in the trilogy of the films had; rather, he had executed a hideous plan with precision, leaving victims screaming, groaning and dead.

The film continued to flash across the big screen, but the spectators were no longer looking for Batman to come back and save the imaginary city. Those who had ducked underneath the seats were terrified of the masked sniper. Some moaned whispers, "Do you think he's coming back?" In the aftermath, survivors bellowed that the dark knight had risen-indeed. A woman who later recounted the massacre said, "I came thinking that good would win over evil, but evil has triumphed again. I will always be on the lookout for evil that lurks in the darkness." (2)

†

I'll say it again, but maybe a little louder. I AM NOT SCARED TO DIE. The perspective I have about God's promise is so clear, whether it's going to concerts, football games or movies. I know what lies

I'M NOT SCARED TO DIE

ahead of me for eternity and who holds it. So let's wake up as Christians, if we REALLY know where we are going. Fear, in the terms of being frightened, should be a word we choose to not understand. I know these are all horrible and devastating things that happen and if you knew me, you know my heart in this, but sometimes I think about the Christians who tragically got murdered in these situations and I say to myself, "They were at a concert or a movie? What a way to go out."

MORE

4

TO THE JOY

"The joy of the Lord is my strength, knowing that He is with me, knowing that He will never leave me, knowing that He is bigger than any circumstance, and that He loves us. It's not about Nick being happy but Nick's trust in God. It is not that everything is going smoothly. It is not that Nick never cries or Nick is never fearful anymore."

-Nick Vujicic

WHEN I FIRST became a Christian it was hard, I was still a train wreck headed towards destruction with a pit stop to get a quad shot of espresso to "cure" this hangover. In the beginning, I was waking up each and every day just trying to figure out why my heart hurts, why this Jesus guy wasn't an instant fix. It was making joy really hard to come by because not only was I still partying and drinking but also I was still doing all the other wrong things. I was disgusted that I was watching pornography still and I was doing all the things in the beginning that you were supposed to be doing, especially after having just been baptized. I know one thing for sure after looking back at all that stuff, I know that God makes all my disappointments into a dance floor. But it wasn't easy and in all honesty I'm glad it wasn't.

†

I want to point out some things that weren't terrible in the beginning. God was working and the joy and the freedom that I found in the first worship song that I ever experienced as a Christian man was Kari Jobes "Forever." Uhg! Tears. She has this awesome twelve minute video on YouTube while right in the middle of the song there was a spoken word artist, Isaac Wimberly that came out and honestly changed my life. Don't be lame and go watch it. But here is the poem that he speaks in the middle of her song in that video.

†

"Words"

If there are words for Him then I don't have them

You see my brain has not yet reached a point

Where it could form a thought

That could adequately describe the greatness of my God

And my lungs have not yet developed the ability

To release a breath with enough agility

To breathe out the greatness of His love

And my voice, my voice is so inhibited

Restrained by human limits

That it's hard to even send a praise up

If there are words for Him then I don't have them

My God

His grace is remarkable

Mercies are innumerable

Strength is impenetrable

He is honorable, accountable, and favorable

Unsearchable yet knowable

Indefinable yet approachable

Indescribable yet personal

He is beyond comprehension

Further than imagination

Constant through generations

King of every nation

But

If there are words for Him then I don't have them

You see my words are few

And to try and capture the one TRUE God

Using my vocabulary will never do
But I use my words as an expression
An expression of worship to a Savior
A Savior who is both worthy and deserving of my praise
So I use words
My heart extols the Lord
Blesses His name forever
He has won my heart, captured my mind
And has bound them both together
He has defeated me in my rebellion
Conquered me in my sin
He has welcomed me into His presence
Completely invited me in
He has made Himself the object of my sight
Flooding me with mercies in the morning
Drowning me with grace in the night
But
If there are words for Him then I don't have them
But what I do have…Is Good News
For my God knew that man-made words would never do
For words are just tools that we use
To point to the Truth
So He sent his son Jesus Christ as THE WORD
Living proof
He is the image of the invisible God
The firstborn of all creation
For by Him all things were created
Giving nothingness formation
And by His word He sustains, in the power of His name

For He is before all things and over all things He reigns
HOLY IS HIS NAME!!
Praise Him for His life
The way He persevered in strife
The humble Son of God becoming the perfect sacrifice
Praise Him for His death
That He willingly stood in our place
That He lovingly endured the grave
That He battled our enemy
And on the third day rose in victory
Praise Him because He rose!!
Hallelujah He rose!!
He is everything that was promised
Praise Him as the risen King
Lift your voice and sing
For one day He will return for us and we will finally be
United with our Savior for eternity
So it's not just words that I proclaim
For my words point to the WORD
And the WORD has a name
Hope has a name
Joy as a name
Peace has a name
Love has a name
And that name is Jesus Christ
Praise His name FOREVER!

†

There's millions and millions of views on that YouTube video and I guarantee you, I'm at least one million of those views. The Holy Spirit just grabs me every time I listen to that song and that poem because the man's voice, his passion, and his gifts are just so powerful. It reaches in my soul and just brings me out of whatever I'm going through. I say, "You know what! God is so good and the enemy is not going to get me!" In that very moment, that's pure joy. The smile that I experience is from the Holy Spirit filling me up, knowing God is with me.

That joy reminds me of my childhood. It reminds me of walking out of my house on a beautiful spring day, walking down to the street corner to meet up with my friends and realizing the special moment when the freezing winter finally turns into spring. That breeze that calms the air, the liveliness going on around, the wind sifting through the trees that start brushing helicopter seeds off the trees. They fall to the ground with such simplicity, such beauty, such amazement that you almost can't help yourself but stop and look at the seeds gracefully falling to the ground and just be in awe. As a kid I always loved those helicopter seeds. I'd grab a handful of them and just throw them up in the air and watch all of them twirl down. It was just so much fun and brought me so much joy because I do believe at a young age I had a love. It may have been small but I had a love for the little things and those helicopter seeds might've been the staple to my childhood.

As simple as that was, it wasn't until I met Christ that I had an understanding of how beautiful God's creation was. Those helicopter seeds seemed so simple until I picked one up and examined the incredible details of just one seed. How many plants could grow from all those seeds? It's hard for me to think about those seeds and not smile, not be filled with joy and be reminded of a passage in the Bible.

"Jesus replied, "The hour has come for the Son of Man to be glorified. Very truly I tell you, unless a kernel of wheat falls to the ground and dies, it remains only a single seed. But if it dies, it produces many seeds. Anyone who loves their life will lose it, while anyone who hates their life in this world will keep it for eternal life. Whoever serves me must follow me; and where I am, my servant also will be. My Father will honor the one who serves me."

John 12:23-26 NIV

Jesus was coming up on his last week of his life in John chapter 12. Entering Jerusalem He acknowledged that He was the Son of God, and He was about to take away the sins of the world. He was accepting praise as

God, but in this passage He was trying to teach us the principle about living for God and bearing a fruitful life. When we follow after God, His purpose, and His plan we'll actually have an abundant life. We will not only bless ourselves, but bless others. So Jesus comes onto the scene saying He has a purpose to fulfill the Father's will and we see this happen on the cross. Right before He dies and says "Not my will Lord but your will be done." This seems absolutely crazy at first but you have to understand that it was for a purpose and there was a reason.

So He gives us this illustration of a seed. Unless the seed goes into the ground and does what it's supposed to do, it won't bear much fruit. This is truly a picture of what Jesus was going to do, how He was going to die for the ransom of many so that we can have life. But he also states that this principle is not just for his life but for all his followers as well. He states in verse 25, "Anyone who loves their life will lose it, while anyone who hates their life in this world will keep it for eternal life." He was talking about surrendering your life and that word surrender is a hard one to swallow. Jesus wanted his disciples to bear much fruit, to follow after God's will and not just their own will. There's a lot of joy and pleasure in following God's will and it seems crazy because we have to die to our own self. When we die to ourselves, we are blessed, just like the helicopter

WE SEE THIS HAPPEN ON THE CROSS

seed has a purpose, we have a purpose to surrender our own will and follow after God.

So just as Jesus surrendered his will to God, so should we. We should bear much fruit for God. The joy in surrendering is indescribable. Hallelujah.

THAN

5

TO THE FUTURE

There is no greater discovery than seeing God as the author of your destiny.

- Ravi Zacharias

Through salvation our past has been forgiven, our present is given meaning, and our future is secured.

- Rick Warren

Surely there is a future, and your hope will not be cut off.

- Proverbs 23:18

SPRINTING TOWARDS the noise, I look left and right making sure I don't get hit by a car. Only having a few minutes to see what was going on, the cheering was overwhelming and I had a feeling I knew what was going on. Running inside like a maniac, again looking left and right and looking insanely lost, I was trying to find the party. With no one in sight I had to be smart and figure it out on my own. Luckily I'm pretty smart and found two double doors and above it said *sanctuary*. "Must be the right place" I thought.. Boom, internal fist pump to myself. Pulling both doors open with each hand, I get blasted with people smiling and worship music filling my heart. The atmosphere was electric and I still didn't know what exactly was going on until boom, a projector screen was mirroring the people getting baptized! Luckily I had made my way to a spot to sit down and watch strangers get baptized into God's family. With my timeframe counting down, I got lucky to see the tail end of people outwardly expressing their commitment to Jesus Christ. Wiping away the tears, I had to get back to my wonderful friends, Sonora and Bekah who were waiting for me. We were headed to a football game and we needed to get cash out of a nearby ATM and it so happened while she was rolling her window down to get some moolah (it's just a cool way of saying money if you didn't know) is when I heard the noise. Quickly, I made a decision after hearing the cheers from the vicinity of the church building across the parking lot. It ended up being the best thing to start off the night; any time I am reminded of how great it was getting baptized and expressing my commitment towards the people I love always brings tears of reminiscing.

BOOM INTERNAL FIST PUMP TO MYSELF

After that moment, as I'm looking out the window driving toward the football game, I definitely looked like an actor trying to not cry, like the ones looking out a train window while its raining outside. Yah know, one of those deep thought moments. Seeing the church baptisms got me thinking about my future, my future as a Christian, my future with Christ, my future pursuing ministry, spending eternity with Him.. What happiness. I could care less about the football game at this point, but man, what a powerful moment, it reminded me about all of chapter one in Peter's first letter to the church, starting at verse 3.

Praise be to the God and Father of our Lord Jesus Christ! In his great mercy he has given us new birth into a living hope through the resurrection of Jesus Christ from the dead, and into an inheritance that can never perish, spoil or fade. This inheritance is kept in heaven for you, who through faith are shielded by God's power until the coming of the salvation that is ready to be revealed in the last time. In all this you greatly rejoice, though now for a little while you may have had to suffer grief in all kinds of trials. These have come so that the proven genuineness of your faith—of greater worth than gold, which perishes even though refined by fire—may result in praise, glory and honor when Jesus Christ is revealed. Though you have not seen him, you love him; and even though you do not see him now, you believe in him and are filled with an inexpressible and glorious joy, for you are receiving the end result of your faith, the salvation of your souls. Concerning this salvation, the prophets, who spoke of the grace that was to come to you, searched intently and with the greatest care, trying to find out the time and circumstances to which the Spirit of Christ in them was pointing when he predicted the sufferings of the Messiah and the glories that would follow. It was revealed to them that they were not serving themselves but you, when they spoke of the things that have now been told you by those who have preached the gospel to you by the Holy Spirit sent from heaven. Even angels long to look into these things.

- 1 Peter 1:3-12

†

I asked a very wise man by the name of Neil Sybert what his thoughts of the future with Christ means to him and he seriously blew my mind. There I was, thinking of the future literally as the days to come, and he brings up a point of his relationship with him TODAY. He said if it wasn't for his pursuit of an intimate relationship with him today and now, then what's the point of thinking about the future? It got me wondering if I'm "worried" about my future with all this thinking that I'm doing, and quickly before I could write another sentence it reminded me what Jesus said in the book of Matthew,

Therefore do not worry about tomorrow, for tomorrow will worry about itself. Each day has enough trouble of its own.
     -Matthew 6:34

So this was my wake up call about worrying, or thinking too much, as I do believe that it will be impossible to be a writer and not think too much. I need to stop thinking about my future with Christ so much. Of course I believe having a "heavenly" mindset is incredibly important to help you along the way of making day-to-day decisions. But my present relationship with Christ is above all, number one on my list. As much fun it is to think about the future of what heaven will be like, I'm going to try (and I hope you will try with me) to practice presence, presence with the Lord TODAY, presence with the people around us and presence in the life we are living right NOW. Because I don't want to see God's working hands in what's happening around me each and everyday if I'm looking at it with my peripherals.

YOU'LL

6

TO THE IMPERFECTIONS

Waking up to the fact that NO ONE and/or ONE'S life is perfect. So don't strive to achieve someone else's perfect life, but take what you have and work with it. Get help if you need it, and trust me….everyone needs help.

-Zoe Lopp

MAN O MAN.. Did I look up to people or what? Did I compare myself to others my entire life? I will ultimately admit that I still do and I think everyone has a simple struggle of comparison. Some might have the ability or maturity in their faith to quickly snap out of comparison mode but most us do it every day and it's a horrible cycle.

"Wish I could speak like him"
"Wish I could be happy like him"
"Wish I had his hair"
"Wish I could lead like him"
"Wish I could worship like him"
"Wish I could sing like him"
"Wish I had that much money"
"Wish I had a wife like him"
"Wish I could dress like him"
"Wish I could be fit like him"

BLAHHHHHH!!! The amount of areas that I can have wishful thinking or have an attitude of jealousy is just endless and it makes me sick to my stomach. The comparison game is ultimately leading to all the insecurities and all the imperfections that I see in myself. The mirror is an ugly and disastrous place sometimes. The reflection can be upsetting and it

THE MIRROR IS AN UGLY AND DISASTROUS PLACE SOMETIMES

can definitely make me think back to times that I literally hated what I saw and wanted to die. But that feeling of disgust leads to the idea of understanding that EVERYONE is struggling with their imperfections. It's primarily up to us to get the world and society's view on us out of our hearts and getting the word of God in them. Begs for for some honest reflection and questions

"But doesn't everyone compare?"
"Is anyone ever fully satisfied with him/herself?"

It's reminds me of a story about Jesus on how he didn't care what society said. He didn't care what the world thought. He didn't care that He was a Jew and she was a Samaritan. He didn't care about anything other than loving this person and telling her the truth about his endless supply of His living water.

John chapter 4 (Take a minute and go read it, I dare you =P) has a simple message about worship, but before the message was delivered we can't bypass the important details of how against the grain of society it was for Jesus to talk to this Samaritan woman. I don't doubt my imagination for a second the amount of times that the Samaritans were playing the comparison game.

"Wish I was a Jew"
"Wish I was good enough"
"Does God even love me if I don't worship in Jerusalem?"
"What's wrong with worshipping on a mountain?"
"Wish I could travel on that road"

When looking past imperfections of people and just insanely loving them as Jesus would, it reminded me of a story of how this teacher, Helen P. Mrosla treated her students. She was explaining her experience with a kid she taught, Mark Eklund. Here is the beautiful story she told:

"One Friday in the classroom things just didn't feel right. We had worked hard on a new concept all week, and I sensed that the students were growing frustrated with themselves and edgy with one another. I had to stop this crankiness before it got out of hand. So I asked them to list the names of the other students in the room on two sheets of paper, leaving a space between each name. Then I told them to think of the nicest thing they could say about each of their classmates and write it down. It took the remainder of the class period to finish the assignment, but as the students left the room, each of them handed me their paper.

That Saturday, I wrote down the name of each student on a separate sheet of paper, and I listed what everyone else had said about that individual. On Monday I gave each student his or her list. Some of them ran two pages. Before long, the entire class was smiling. "Really?" I heard whispered. "I never knew that meant anything to anyone!" "I didn't know others liked me so much!"

No one ever mentioned those papers in class again. I never knew if they discussed them after class or with their parents, but it didn't matter. The exercise had accomplished its purpose. The students were happy with themselves and one another again.

That group of students moved on. Several years later, after I had returned from a vacation, my parents met me at the airport. As we were driving home, Mother asked the usual questions about the trip: How the weather was, my experience in general. There was a slight lull in the conversation. Mother gave Dad a sideways glance and simply said, "Dad?" My father cleared his throat. "The Eklunds called last night," he began.

"Really?" I said. "I haven't heard from them in several years. I wonder how Mark is."

Dad responded quietly. "Mark was killed in Vietnam," he said. "The funeral is tomorrow, and his parents would like it if you could attend." To this day I can still point to the exact spot on I-494 where Dad told me about Mark.

I had never seen a serviceman in a military coffin before. The church was packed with Mark's friends. His old classmate, Chuck's sister, sang "The Battle Hymn of the Republic." Why did it have to rain on the day of the funeral? It was difficult enough at the graveside. The pastor said the usual prayers and the bugler played taps. One by one those who loved Mark took a last walk by the coffin and sprinkled it with holy water.

I was the last one to bless the coffin. As I stood there, one of the soldiers who had acted as a pallbearer came up to me. "Were you Mark's math teacher?" he asked. I nodded as I continued to start at the coffin. "Mark talked about you a lot," he said.

After the funeral, most of Mark's former classmates headed to Chuck's farmhouse for lunch. Mark's mother and father were there, obviously waiting for me. "We want to show you something," his father said, taking a wallet out of his pocket. "They found this on Mark when he was killed. We thought you might recognize it."

Opening the billfold, he carefully removed two worn pieces of notebook paper that had obviously been taped, folded and refolded many time. I knew without looking that the papers were the ones on which I had listed all the good things each of Mark's classmates had said about him. "Thank you so much for doing that," Mark's mother said. "As you can see, Mark treasured it."

Mark's classmates started to gather around us. Chuck smiled rather sheepishly and said, "I still have my list. It's in the top drawer of my desk at home." John's wife said, "John asked me to put his in our wedding album." "I have mine too," Marilyn said. "It's in my diary." Then Vicky, another classmate, reached into her pocketbook, took out her wallet and showed her worn and frazzled list to the group. "I carry this with me at all times," Vicky said without batting an eyelash. "I think we all saved our lists."

That's when I finally sat down and cried. (3)

So instead of looking at the imperfections of oneself or others, my goodness gracious! Try to find the great things. Bypass the negative and see the beauty. Do

BYPASS THE NEGATIVE AND SEE THE BEAUTY

something amazing with your words, making a moment for people to remember. Do you think that Samaritan woman EVER forgot what Jesus did and said to her? I'd bet you a million dollars (that I do not have) that she didn't. Just his actions spoke volumes. His words changed her life forever, just like this teacher changed her students' life. Imperfections and comparison is a deadly trap and the only way to escape from it is the blood of Jesus. Never forget that your identity comes from God and what his Son did on the cross. I know it's hard... I struggle with it every dang day.. But that doesn't change the fact that I NEED to understand that picking up my cross daily is a necessity that should never be taken lightly. Wake up to seeing the good...no, not just the good, but the best in people. Look at that reflection and see yourself and others the way Jesus does.

EVER

7

TO FAITH

Faith isn't a feeling. It's a choice to trust God even when the road ahead seems uncertain.

-Dave Willis

LOOKING OUT the window, it was a warm and musky summer day, as we pull into a parking spot in God knows where. I figured out that I was in Lodi, California, not knowing where that was, nor did I care. I was too distracted after looking up into the sky and seeing people parachute down and land on this grass field, not fully realizing what I was about to do. I knew that today's trip was going to be the scariest thing that I've ever had to do. I was going to have to strap my body to a complete stranger, trust him with my precious life, and jump out of an airplane at 13,000 feet. Like what??? At this point in my life, I was terrified of heights. Even Mr. Toad's roller coaster at Disneyland scared me. I was terrified of anything that I didn't have complete control over and sky-diving was perfect, I could control *everything*...NOT! It was a perfect example of like, "HEY DUMBO" you do not have any control over the parachute, the wind, the plane or the near-death experience that is about to take place because this complete stranger that you strap yourself to you has the controls. Yea, smart move bro.

Long story short, I died.

Just kidding, but in reality, thinking back to that moment and experience had me thinking about how faith in God works exactly the same way. We decide to trust God with our lives, just as I did with the stranger directing my parachute. Trust me. It can be scary but when we figure out that we have a professional attached to us, the mood gets a little lighter. I'm not saying trusting God and putting your complete life on the line for him is easy but what other options do we have? Are you, as a Christian willing to jump out into his arms, trusting him with everything that you feel like you don't have control of? Because life will hit you with things or situations that you feel you don't have any say toward the outcome, you can't change a thing. But jumping out of that airplane knowing from past experiences that I made it out okay, is the perfect example of why I can trust God with any situation. That's real faith, faith that God will bring me out of anything, knowing from the past that He's done it before. Some people call it a blind leap of faith but the Bible and my life is full of stories that God has come through again and again. So what am I scared of? Check out what the Bible says about the God we follow:

For the word of the Lord is right and true;

he is faithful in all he does.

The Lord loves righteousness and justice;

the earth is full of his unfailing love.

By the word of the Lord the heavens were made,

their starry host by the breath of his mouth.

Psalm 33:4-6 NIV

There's simply not a better decision I have ever made than to surrender to the will of God and trust Him with my life. I understand His plans are so much better than mine and all I have to do is jump out of the plane. Waking up to not only the idea but the truth that if and when you decide to jump out of the airplane, he will welcome you right into his loving arms. This has to be one of my favorite quotes:

"Give me all of you! I don't want so much of your time, so much of your talents and money, and so much of your work. I want YOU!!! ALL OF YOU!! I have not come to torment or frustrate the natural man or woman, but to KILL IT! No half measures will do. I don't want to only prune a branch here and a branch there; rather I want the whole tree out! Hand it over to me, the whole outfit, all of your desires, all of your wants and wishes and dreams. Turn them ALL over to me, give yourself to me and I will make of you a new self---in my image. Give me yourself and in exchange I will give you Myself. My will, shall become your will. My heart, shall become your heart."

-C.S. Lewis, Mere Christianity

As it approaches midnight, I'm writing this. I laughed so hard thinking about this and I just decided to go with this crazy analogy of surrendering everything. This is how funny writers can be sometimes, and that's what's cool about writing. There are no rules and that's just the way I like it baby, so here yah go. It's not like you can jump out of the airplane with only your arm or a leg or maybe you can just leave your torso on the plane and watch and see if the other body parts safely land on the ground to then think about jumping. The Bible says you must sacrifice everything.

Then Jesus said to His disciples, "If anyone wishes to come after Me, he must deny himself, and take up his cross and follow Me. For whoever wishes to save his life will lose it; but whoever loses his life for My sake will find it."

Matthew 16:24-25

It costs everything to actually have faith in our God. It makes us leave all our desires, wants, regrets, guilt, shame and decisions on that plane. We must grab a parachute and jump into full submission of God's will. The breath of fresh air, the ability to see the beautiful life that God has for you and the thrill of landing, realizing that decision to jump was not easy but worth it. Most of us who are reading this book have a relationship with Christ and can relate to this confusing, yet truthful analogy. But if you don't and have seemed to come this far. Don't think about it. Just jump.

KNOW

8

TO THE GOOD

Every good and perfect gift is from above, coming down from the Father of the heavenly lights, who does not change like shifting shadows.

- James 1:17 NIV

"How are you?"
"Good, how are you?"
"Well why are you good?"

- Mackenzie Benson

I HAVE THIS particular weird thing that I do. And when I say weird it's because most people get either a stalker vibe or they are just completely caught off guard. At any coffee shop or restaurant or anywhere else when someone asks me how I'm doing, I say how I'm doing and then in short I ask them how they're doing and most of the time they say "I'm good", and then I follow up with "Why are you good?" Most of the time a cliché answer comes out like,

"Well, I'm breathing today."
"Well, I have a job."
 "Well, life is good, that's why."

But on occasion I get a real answer.. And in all honesty.. I love it when people are real.. That's when I can actually pray for them. And I've done that for years, I've prayed for people, I've invited people to church and I've done some cool things with that little conversation starter. Mackenzie was a junior high girl that I saw grow up into a high school student, and when I was sitting in the church's coffee shop writing, she came up to me and asked me how I was doing, and I said,

"I'm good. How are you?"

She looked straight in my eyes and said,

"Well, why are you good?"

At first I thought, "Hey that's my thing!" Of course I had to shove my huge ego aside, realizing how cool it was that such a caring attitude came from someone so young. It was beautiful. I wish you could've seen the look in her eyes. She truly cared.

       This reminds me of another time where I was interrupted politely. Heck, this particular time I wasn't writing anything. Writer's block sucks; it's wasted time I spend daydreaming about being done with my current project or of a time where I was actually motivated.

       Maybe calling it "writer's block" is my excuse to get me out of calling myself lazy or unmotivated. It always seems to come at the perfect time in being, not the perfect time at all. Because at this very moment I had planned to write and I got excited to write. This is ironic, but I was energized to *sit down* and get in the zone. It's ironic because I'm a fitness guy and getting pumped to sit down is something I'll never get used to doing. But seriously, as a writer I have to get excited to plop my booty down.

This particular night I was sitting in front of the church coffeehouse. Yes, this church has its own coffeehouse. I work at an amazing place, North Coast Church. You should check it out. When it closes, I don't get sad because I can easily just pop outside and sit at the tables outside and keep grinding away. There are even outlets and Wi-Fi! So I've caught myself writing until midnight some nights because duh, San Diego weather is perfect. As I get re-situated to write, I take a glimpse of our beautiful church campus, the way they have strung the lights to make me feel like I'm at a wedding. They've perfected the theme with the palm trees and fountains to let me know that I'm spoiled and have nothing to complain about, except this writer's block.

An older gentleman, complete stranger, interrupted me in a very calm tone,

"Hey, are you working or are you chilling?"

I instantly thought to myself,

"How did he know I wasn't doing anything productive?! He's a wizard."

"I'm actually.."

Before I could tell him the truth of my laziness, he sat down.

I'm a guy who always was open to real conversation and meeting new people was typically a breeze because the word shy is not in my dictionary. We immediately opened up about real things about God and life. It was, simply put, just beautiful. A life of making huge mistakes with alcohol and drugs turned into one full of Jesus and music. Talking about music ended up being the spark to a very memorable night. We learned that both of us have a passion for the guitar so he left to get his guitar from his car. He also brought a harmonica and we literally started a band, right then and there in the church plaza, straight jamming. I wouldn't want to be anywhere else in the whole world at that moment, but it got better. We decided to brag on social media a bit about our band. Bryce, a wonderful friend of mine, rushed over and joined us with his mini drum kit. We took turns on different instruments, played our hearts out and laughed until being kicked out by the security guard, thus ending the career aspirations of our band.

†

The reason I tell these simple stories is because I don't want to be too busy with what's going on or what I'm working on to miss the conversations. Conversations that can lead to memories or to new friendships. Thinking back to my moment of realization that I needed God in my life, it all started with conversations: conversations about the goodness of God, conversations of salvation, conversations with other believers. Who knows where I'd be without those crucial talks in my life. I'm waking up to the idea that I don't ever want to miss the opportunity to talk from the heart, setting technology and the fast-paced lifestyle aside. I have this thing, (I have a lot of *things*) that if I sit next to someone at a coffee shop, or on an airplane or anywhere else, I just introduce myself. That way, I don't feel like I'm sitting next to a complete stranger. I know most people don't care, but I do. Sometimes that sparks some real amazing conversations. So don't be too busy to have a conversation. Honestly, it might be way more important than what you're actually doing.

THINK

9

TO THE TRUTH

Our feelings are real and powerful, but they are not more powerful than God and the Truth

-Joyce Meyer

Jesus answered, "I am the way and the truth and the life. No one comes to the Father except through me.

-John 14:6 (NIV)

I'M STEPPING ONTO this massive bird. I've never   seen a plane this big. Walking through the aisles trying to find my seat, I don't even know that there's a row that corresponds to each letter in the alphabet, and then some. I walked for what seemed to be an hour and still upset that I didn't get the first class section because it looked like they got beds for this 13-hour flight. Yes, I said it. 13 hours from the Los Angeles airport to Tel Aviv, Israel with a pit stop in Istanbul, Turkey. This trip was going to be the trip of an absolute lifetime. I was on fire. I was ready to walk what they call the Holy Land and walk where Jesus walked. I sat in my chair, waiting for my knees to start hurting from being crammed into such a tight space. I'm not a gigantic human but I'm not small either. Six foot-one was the perfect length to where my knees rest against the folding tray table, which is a nice little rest until your sick of metal going into your knee cap. I did the obvious: buckled up and started to look around at all the people in my vicinity. I was lucky enough to be sitting next to two of my favorite people, a part of our group from the North Coast Church School of Ministry.

There were about twenty of us, pumped up, eager, and ready to learn be Christ followers by way of this big ole bird. We were ready to fly across the world. Siting by Chelle and Lo was the only way I got through this 13-hour disaster, but let's get real for a second. I'm never opposed to 13 hours of doing nothing but reading, talking, listening to music and watching movies. So the story telling, starting movies at the exact time on our personal, airplane provided iPads and talking about it after was fun. We were simply the three best friends anyone could ask for. (Chelle, thanks so much for the pictures, seriously. Lo, keep smiling and keep climbing. I miss you two.)

I've always been an impulse guy. When I'm interested in something, or if there's something that I can aspire to be better at, it's quite fortunate and unfortunate at the same time. Meaning, I learn things quickly, but often times it has led to dumb financial purchases or wasted time. Without a doubt it's led to more fortunate situations over unfortunate. But the dumb ones still sting. So this trip was nothing short of a miracle from God. First off, I NEEDED to go and there was nothing that was going to stop me from obtaining the trip fare of three thousand dollars. So I do what everyone does, ask people for money. Okay, so maybe most people aren't as desperate as I was about this trip, but I made an account on a crowd funding site (where people can donate to your cause, in this case my "cause" was "Send Zack to Israel") Regardless if you agree with this method or not, it happened and I was already sweating on this gigantic airplane with anxiety and excitement about the truth. Jesus was already in my heart, but I was ready to SEE it.

Evidence is hard to spell, I used an "s" instead of a "c" like three times typing this sentence, which is why I'm laughing so hard, but even though it took me longer than it should've to type the word evidence, it takes people a lifetime to understand the word. There's something that gets in the way. Is it pride? Disillusionment? Insecurities? Who knows, but I'm no man of perfection. I was a man who once said, "People who need God are too weak to want it by themselves." So that word evidence after being a Christian for a short two years was something I dove in HARD. Picture me diving into a Wal-Mart kiddy pool from the roof, risking breaking every bone in my body doing so, but there it was, the catch.. I was heartbroken at the time and could care less about what I'd break because no pain surpasses the pain of a crushed spirit and smashed heart. I wanted truth; I wanted reasoning why my heart was so transformed by what my savior Jesus did for me on that cross. This trip was about to be, not the cherry on top, but the whole dessert menu. I was already on fire, I fell in love with the story of the Bible. So that's why I decided to go see it, to back it ALL UP.

†

A slight breeze was coming from each direction as I stood up from catching my breath. Sweat was pouring down my face and I was fist bumping one of my best friends, Bryan Hall. We did it! We were staring at the sun rising on the Sea of Galilee in Israel, with worship music playing from my headphones. I couldn't think of a better feeling, nor did I want to. It takes a special breed of a human to workout during a trip or vacation, but I took pride in being a little crazy and being a part of that lifestyle. But wow, could I not be more thankful for

THERE IT WAS, THE SEA OF GALILEE, WHERE JESUS WALKED, WHERE PETER HAD LITTLE FAITH my roommate Bryan, one of those crazy humans too! We just ran along the beach of the Sea of Galilee and threw rocks on our shoulders and did some thrusters (it's a CrossFit thing, Google it.) But there it was, the Sea of Galilee, where Jesus walked and where Peter had little faith. I'm seeing it, I'm feeling the water, and I'm seeing the surrounding cities and beautiful mountains. The story in Matthew just became that much more real, that much more believable.

Immediately Jesus made the disciples get into the boat and go on ahead of him to the other side, while he dismissed the crowd. After he had dismissed them, he went up on a mountainside by himself to pray. Later that night, he was there alone, and the boat was already a considerable distance from land, buffeted by the waves because the wind was against it. Shortly before dawn Jesus went out to them, walking on the lake. When the disciples saw him walking on the lake, they were terrified. "It's a ghost," they said, and cried out in fear.

But Jesus immediately said to them: "Take courage! It is I. Don't be afraid."

"Lord, if it's you," Peter replied, "tell me to come to you on the water."

"Come," he said.

Then Peter got down out of the boat, walked on the water and came toward Jesus. But when he saw the wind, he was afraid and, beginning to sink, cried out, "Lord, save me!"

Immediately Jesus reached out his hand and caught him. "You of little faith," he said, "why did you doubt?"

And when they climbed into the boat, the wind died down. Then those who were in the boat worshiped him, saying, "Truly you are the Son of God."

Matthew 14:22-33 NIV

From walking around in Jerusalem to walking up Mt. Arbel where Jesus prayed after feeding the five-thousand and overlooking the sea of Galilee. This Bible study trip was nothing short of amazing. But there was one moment that struck me, one experience that locked in the idea so hard that I want to teach this story for the rest of my life. It's found in Mark 1:21 and it says this.

"They went to Capernaum, and when the Sabbath came, Jesus went into the synagogue and began to teach." (NIV)

It's an easy verse to understand. It's a verse that sets the scene when Jesus would perform a miracle of driving out an impure spirit. But there's something special about this. It's where Jesus was located during this particular teaching and miracle. They went to Capernaum and began to teach at the synagogue, guess where we were? Yup, at that same synagogue in Capernaum. I got the opportunity of a lifetime, to read that verse and story at the same synagogue, in the same city where Jesus ACTUALLY taught that gives me chills and a stomach drop happens every single time I think about it.

†

I can go deeply into every single detail about our trip, and I often say to myself, "I wish I could send everyone to Israel to see what I saw. Then they will believe." Most of us know that's not how it works. Even when people see the evidence, their hearts and minds won't get changed because they love their

IT MADE MY BIBLE A COLOR 3-D POPUP STORY BOOK

lifestyle of sin too much. As a believing Christian, I recommend you go. It was such an affirmation trip that woke every ounce of my being up; it made my Bible a color 3-D pop up storybook. I smile from ear to ear whenever I read a passage that takes place at a location that I've actually physically been to. It made my perspective of truth so clear; there's no grey area with the way I feel and believe in the Bible. I've felt the Holy Spirit and had faith that God has done and will do what He says, and I've also seen the actually physical evidence of it all.

The Bible contains the mind of God, the state of man, the way of salvation, the doom of sinners, and the happiness of believers. Its doctrines are holy, its precepts are binding, its histories are true, and its decisions are immutable. Read it to be wise, believe it to be safe, and practice it to be holy. It contains light to direct you, food to support you, and comfort to cheer you. It is the traveler's map, the pilgrim's staff, the pilot's compass, the soldier's sword and the Christian's charter. Here too, Heaven is opened and the gates of Hell disclosed. Christ is its grand subject, our good its design, and the glory of God its end. It should fill the memory, rule the heart and guide the feet. Read it slowly, frequently and prayerfully. It is a mine of wealth, a paradise of glory, and a river of pleasure. It is given you in life, will be opened at the judgment, and be remembered forever. It involves the highest responsibility, rewards the greatest labor, and will condemn all who trifle with its sacred contents.

-The Gideons International.

OR

10

TO THE GOOD

To gather with God's people in united adoration of the Father is as necessary to the Christian life as prayer.

- Martin Luther

GOD DIDN'T put us on this earth with however many billion people to do life alone. One thing that I've really loved waking up to is the idea of being with, doing life with and interacting with people: Fellowship, building with people, experiencing people and loving people. Writing this book without people and with just my own inspiration is a joke. I'm waking up to understand that people are awesome. There are intelligent people wherever you look. There are huge-hearted, incredible women and men of God, inspirational people who have helped me throughout the whole process of writing this book. Also in a way, they've helped me wake up to the ability to actually listen: listening to other people's opinions, ideas, goals, dreams, and stories. Because man-o-man, you sure can learn, grow, achieve and mature a lot once you get yourself out of the way. I think that's God's way of saying, "Hey y'all are connected into one big family. Listen and understand that you can't do it alone". (And yes God said *y'all* all the time)

The way I see it, living in the dark and living in sin and refusing to accept God's truth is a lot like sleeping. The day you "wake up" is the day you'll be awake for the rest of your life. That day or moment that someone important enters your life and shares the truth with you in a way that resonates with you, or the day that you decide to go to church reluctantly but with an open mind and hear a message that just clicks, or the instant you feel that conviction and know something needs to change, that aha! moment, that's the moment you wake up. That's the alarm clock. But sometimes an alarm clock isn't enough. You look at your life and you say, "I think things are going pretty good for me just the way they are. Why would I want to change my whole life around when I get to do whatever I want?" And so you hear that alarm clock go off, and you press snooze, over and over again and you sleep your day away. You know you're not going to get anything productive done. You're wasting precious time that you could be using to work toward your goals, dreams and aspirations. You could be launched into a whirlwind of new and incredible opportunities that you never expected or could have dreamed of, but you're tired, so you press snooze. But before you roll over and go back to sleep, just do this for me; go ahead and ask anyone who has been awake for a while, and I promise you they will be able to tell you all about the day that their alarm clock went off, and how they stared at it for a long while, contemplating hitting that snooze button. They might even tell you about someone who came alongside them and helped them get up, got them dressed and brewed them a cup of coffee. And they will probably tell you it wasn't easy. But I can also assure you that they will say once they were up and had that first sip of coffee in the morning, they knew they were right where they were supposed to be.

God isn't promising any of us an easy life, but He is promising a perfect eternal life. So maybe you'll get up and wish you hadn't, and maybe you'll even get a flat tire on the way to work. But when you get to sit down and watch the sunset at the end of the day with your loved ones, it'll be really hard to say it wasn't worth it.

So wake up. Because if you never wake up, you might sleep through some of the hard stuff, but I promise you'll miss all the good stuff too."

-Marysa Kamps

The last bone-shaking, chills-inducing, eye-opening line of that beautiful message my friend wrote is just jaw dropping. "So wake up, because if you never wake up, you might sleep through some of the hard stuff,

ALL I DO IS TRY MY BEST TO SPREAD THE STORIES OF MY AWAKENING, MY REVIVAL, MY SALVATION

but I promise you'll miss all the good stuff too." I don't know about you, but I definitely don't want to miss the good stuff God has for me in this life. The smile-producing stuff, the jump in the air and shout "I'M ALIVE" stuff, the seeing God work in amazing ways stuff. The waking up that has to happen in order to experience God's grace and mercy is the Holy Spirit's job, not mine. All I do is try my best to spread the stories of my awakening, my revival, my salvation, in hopes that maybe you will say a prayer to invite the Holy Spirit in and ask God to open your eyes and heart to the freedom He offers. But just wait a minute.. Don't forget that we have to be ready, equipped and not be shaken from the evil of this world. Because as much as I'd love this walk with Jesus Christ to be filled with joy and cheeseburgers all the time, there's people dying, evil people murdering and a real spiritual battle happening today.

I fought with myself about putting an invitation in this book and ultimately I said, "Why not?" Waking up to how glorious fellowshipping with God's family is was the best thing that has ever happened to me. There might be some of you reading this who aren't truly in the family of God, or confused on how to get in or, better yet, don't know how to lead someone. Let me help. Here is the Gospel in four verses and the road to salvation following it, known as "Romans Road" in again, four verses.

Genesis 1:1 says: In the beginning God created the heavens and the earth. (NIV)
Having an understanding that God created everything is crucial. Everything we see, smell, and taste. The Creator created all. Touch and taste.

John 1:1 says: In the beginning was the word, and the word was with God and the word was God.(NIV)
In the beginning it clearly states that the Word (Jesus) was there when He created everything.

John 1:14 says: The Word became flesh and made his dwelling among us.(NIV)
The Word (Jesus) came down as a man and lived among us humans.

John 3:16 says: For God so loved the world that He sent His one and only son, so that whoever believes in Him, shall not perish but have eternal life. (NIV)
God the creator loved earth and us so much that he sent the Word (Jesus) to earth to live a perfect and sinless life to

die for us on the cross. Then God raised Jesus from the dead, giving us freedom from sin and breaking every chain of shame and guilt.

Now that is the long story short of the Gospel of Jesus Christ in four verses! How exciting! If you didn't know of this man dying for you, now you do! Someone was literally beaten, scarred and killed for YOU. What a sacrifice! But we aren't done yet! Let me explain to you why we needed this man Jesus Christ to die for all of us and how to receive his sacrifice in our heart. And from there we can start living a life dedicated to Him full of purpose, passion and blessings.

Romans 3:23 says: For we have all sinned and fallen short of the glory of God.
That verse is talking to each one of us, that we all have this sinful nature that falls short of what God originally designed. We are all sinners!

Romans 6:23 says: For the wages of sin is death! But the gift from God is eternal life in Christ Jesus.
Sin is nasty and without the sacrifice of Jesus we would all die in our ways of selfishness and living a life for ourselves. But God gave us a gift! And that gift is in his Son Jesus! That's good news!

Romans 5:8 says: But God demonstrates His love for us in this: While we were still sinners Christ died for us.

What love! While we were still stuck in our sin without a way out, Jesus died for us! That was the plan all along! What a God!

Romans 10:9 says: If you declare with your mouth that Jesus is Lord and that God raised him from the dead you will be saved.

I want to use the word "simple" very carefully here. Yes it is simple to understand if we say that Jesus is Lord and believe in our heart that God raised Him from the dead that we will be saved. But to really believe in your heart could be easier said than done. Take some time to think about this. There should be no doubt in your heart or mind that this is true.

Okay, so I definitely know how much that was to take in within a couple minutes. But truly I tell you, there might not be any other verses that are more important than those eight I just went over. They told us about creation, what God did, who Jesus was, how to understand and fully receive Him, and what He did for us on that cross. What an amazing story, right? Do me a favor. If this is something you

GENESIS 1:1
JOHN 1:1
JOHN 1:14
JOHN 3:16
ROMANS 3:23
ROMANS 6:23
ROMANS 5:8
ROMANS 10:9

want more info on, ask a friend who is a Christian. I'm sure you know of at least one and if you don't, go to a local church. BELIEVE ME, PLEASE, when I tell you that there are Christians out there who want nothing more than to help you understand the verses you just read. Everyone needs help. Just ask.

And for those of you who already call Jesus your Lord and savior, here's a challenge. I'm a big fan of verse memorization and I promise you, memorizing the entire gospel in four verses and the road to salvation comes in handy in pretty much any apologetic situation or when you are telling someone about Jesus. Take a week to memorize those eight verses and I promise fruit will come out of it. People need to know. People need to know how much you care about them. People need to know how much God cares about them. People need to know what Jesus Christ did for them.

IMAGINE

11

TO CONTENMENT

Happy moments **PRAISE GOD**
Difficult moments **SEEK GOD**
Quiet moments, **WORSHIP GOD**
Painful Moments, **TRUST GOD**
Every moment, **THANK GOD**
-Rick Warren

SHIFTED IN PARK. Taking deep breathes, I tried to park away from the direction of any lights that would make an annoying appearance through my windows. Taking my retractable windshield cover that blocks the sun during the day, I used for the remaining lights peaking through. The next part was grabbing the lever to my steering wheel and pulling on it and pushing the steering wheel up as much as I could to clear some room. It was only a few inches but nowadays every inch matters. This situation sucked but I knew it was the right thing to do.. Or did I? Heck, it was the only thing I could do, moving across the country once again is never an easy thing to do, but one thing I did know, it was all going to be worth it.

Grabbing two full size pillows and putting them flat on the floorboards where my feet would go, I fit them perfectly between the front of my driver's seat and the gas pedal. I had to raise the space so my legs wouldn't just dangle and get numb. As I pulled the lever back to lean my chair back as far as it will go, I had done my best to make a bed inside my car. Making sure no one was around to see me being homeless, I tried to find parking spots during the night that I knew wouldn't be disturbed. Have the cops and people knocked on my window to see if I was alive? Yes, and by them doing that, they scared me so much that they themselves could have actually killed me. Honestly, I knew this was going to be a temporary thing, but it actually really upset me when the cops would tell me to get up and leave, knowing ABSOLUTELY I wasn't going to harm or do anything. But then again, I get it, and I got over it really quick.

As I'm writing this in a Starbuck's again in San Diego, California, I am still homeless and I've been living in my car for two months now. It has taught me nothing more than to be content. Honestly I'm the happiest I have ever been. I hope by the time that this book is published that my living situation is different, but as of right now, it's not. And I'm okay with that. I recently just moved back to San Diego from Oklahoma and it was the best thing that could ever happen to me. I pursued an awesome opportunity to work for a church in Oklahoma but ultimately returned to where my heart was in San Diego at a church I was interning for before I left. Usually when someone interns for a church/company, nine times out ten, they want to work for that particular place. But there just wasn't an opportunity at the moment I got the offer from the church in Oklahoma. So I took it and left, only to have a conversation with my dear friends from San Diego the Muche family. Melissa and Bryan worked for the church that I wanted to be a part of and it so happened that a position opened up. Long story short, I took it. And within a year of leaving, I was already heading back, but there was a huge sacrifice awaiting me.

If you know anybody who pursues ministry, they are probably not doing it for the money. The entry level position that I received at my dream church was not enough money to pay rent in San Diego, so I decided I

HAVE YOU EVER WANTED SOMETHING SO BAD THAT YOU WERE LITERALLY WILLING TO SACRIFICE EVERYTHING FOR?

wasn't going to. And still at this moment I can't help to note that there's NO WAY I would put this in my book if I weren't filled with complete joy. Have you ever wanted something so bad that you were literally willing to sacrifice everything for? Your comfort? Your sleep? Your food? That's what I did, I trusted that God was going to take care of my every need and He has so far. So that's where my true understanding of being content comes from. My favorite story in the Bible of being content is when the apostle Paul explained his understanding of contentment in his letter to the Philippians.

"I'm glad in God, far happier than you would ever guess—happy that you're again showing such strong concern for me. Not that you ever quit praying and thinking about me. You just had no chance to show it. Actually, I don't have a sense of needing anything personally. I've learned by now to be quite content whatever my circumstances. I'm just as happy with little as with much, with much as with little. I've found the recipe for being happy whether full or hungry, hands full or hands empty. Whatever I have, wherever I am, I can make it through anything in the One who makes me who I am. I don't mean that your help didn't mean a lot to me—

it did. It was a beautiful thing that you came alongside me in my troubles."

Philippians 4:10-14 The Message (MSG)

Being content is insanely easier said than done, but being a follower of Jesus Christ, it's nothing short of something I want to accomplish. With Paul being content in every situation and any circumstance, it's a lot easier to look at the scriptures and be okay with the mission I'm on. Seriously, just take a look at what he has gone through spreading the gospel in 2 Corinthians 11:23-29. *(In this particular passage the context is about the apostle Paul boasting about his sufferings so I urge you to take a peak of the letter to the Corinthians. But for the sake of contentment, I just want you to see what he has gone through.)*

"Let me come back to where I started—and don't hold it against me if I continue to sound a little foolish. Or if you'd rather, just accept that I am a fool and let me rant on a little. I didn't learn this kind of talk from Christ. Oh, no, it's a bad habit I picked up from the three-ring preachers that are so popular these days. Since you sit there in the judgment seat observing all these shenanigans, you can afford to humor an occasional fool who happens along. You have such admirable tolerance for impostors who rob your freedom, rip you off, steal you blind, put you down—even slap your face! I shouldn't admit it to

you, but our stomachs aren't strong enough to tolerate that kind of stuff.

Since you admire the egomaniacs of the pulpit so much (remember, this is your old friend, the fool, talking), let me try my hand at it. Do they brag of being Hebrews, Israelites, the pure race of Abraham? I'm their match. Are they servants of Christ? I can go them one better. (I can't believe I'm saying these things. It's crazy to talk this way! But I started, and I'm going to finish.)

I've worked much harder, been jailed more often, beaten up more times than I can count, and at death's door time after time. I've been flogged five times with the Jews' thirty-nine lashes, beaten by Roman rods three times, pummeled with rocks once. I've been shipwrecked three times, and immersed in the open sea for a night and a day. In hard traveling year in and year out, I've had to ford rivers, fend off robbers, struggle with friends, struggle with foes. I've been at risk in the city, at risk in the country, endangered by desert sun and sea storm, and betrayed by those I thought were my brothers. I've known drudgery and hard labor, many a long and lonely night without sleep, many a missed meal, blasted by the cold, naked to the weather.

And that's not the half of it, when you throw in the daily pressures and anxieties of all the churches. When someone gets to the end of his rope, I feel the desperation in my bones. When someone is duped into sin, an angry fire burns in my gut.

If I have to "brag" about myself, I'll brag about the humiliations that make me like Jesus. The eternal and blessed God and Father of our Master Jesus knows I'm not lying. Remember the time I was in Damascus and the governor of King Aretas posted guards at the city gates to arrest me? I crawled through a window in the wall, was let down in a basket, and had to run for my life."

2 Corinthians 11:16-33 The Message (MSG)

So regardless of what my life situation is, the waking up to what contentment in Christ really means is that my home is not here on earth. My treasures are not a part of this world. Does the enemy attack all the dang time? Yes, sometimes being lonely is all I feel. Embarrassment is often triggered and the shame creeps in. It's a lot to sacrifice but it won't be forever. Whatever situation you have yourself in, in this beautiful life, waking up to being content is what I'm praying for. At work, with your family, in your relationships, just knowing that you will be okay, if you fully trust and fully follow Christ, your heart will be at ease and peace will be in your soul knowing that God has you.

†

"Why didn't you ask? Did you not have any friends? Why didn't you reach out to your church?" Some of you might disagree with the decision I made about living in my car. But I really found some freedom in this situation and I was just fine. The sufficiency that Christ gives me is something I really live out, and it gives me peace, knowing that I'm not attached to things in life because I'm waking up to the idea that I'm not promised tomorrow, at all. The apostle Paul really understood that for him and this life, Christ was enough. He was in prison and he was fine. He could have nothing and be fine. Paul really took what Jesus said about, not storing things of this earth where moths and rust can get them, but instead putting treasures in heaven.

Be Content, God promises satisfaction will come to those who seek the good things of God. He says that they will be filled. Not with material goods of this world, not with an easy way of life, not with something of limited value that can be taken away from them, but with the joy and contentment that comes from doing Gods will. The filled people are the truly happy people in life.
-Colleen Townsend Evans

JUST

12

TO KNOWLEDGE

Blessed are those who find wisdom,
those who gain understanding,
for she is more profitable than silver
and yields better returns than gold.
She is more precious than rubies;
nothing you desire can compare with her.
Long life is in her right hand;
in her left hand are riches and honor.
Her ways are pleasant ways,
and all her paths are peace.
She is a tree of life to those who take hold of her;
those who hold her fast will be blessed.

-Proverbs 3:13-18 (NIV)

I LAUGH and cry at the same time when I tell people that in my first book *Be Brave,* you can take the combined words and letters written in that book and it probably overtakes the number of words and pages I've written in my whole educational career as a college drop out. As a person who hated school, I thought sitting in school was a waste of time, especially learning things I had no interest in. I consistently hated teachers, hated projects, hated the fact that I had to sit down and type a paper about stuff that I necessarily never cared about or never would care about. I definitely said, "I'll never use this in the future so I'm not doing it," about one hundred times, which ultimately led me to getting a lot of those big ole' "F's" on my transcript.

But in all honesty...once I met Christ, all I did was want to know more, I wanted to learn more. I wanted to read the Bible, I wanted to read every pastor's book, I wanted every perspective. I wanted to learn so much about Who this Jesus guy was. This man changed my life, changed my views about everything..

So as a person who wanted more, I decided to enroll in my church's school of ministry and we had a project to do after year one. We got to talk and write about what things we learned. I decided to write a letter to my "past" self, regarding what lies ahead. This is what is says

A LETTER TO MY 26 YEAR OLD SELF

You need to just do it. As many times as you've failed to be a part of any educational system, this can be redemption. From only getting to walk that stage at your

high school graduation because Nevada had offered you a position on their football team, you know you didn't have the grades nor the determination. God forbid a teacher screws that up. Of course you know that you dropped out of college because beer and women were too important. School was never good for you, nor did you care.

Just submit your application man. What's the worst thing that can happen? A simple no would rid you another "drop out," "quitter" addition to your life's resume. But this felt different and you knew it. You knew this Jesus guy was real, you knew that if you wanted to pursue him you needed help, you needed guidance. Come on, you moved away from home with your truck, a mattress, three hundred dollars and not knowing anybody. You did that. Now just press send. Gods got this.

This North Coasts School of Ministry is going to change your life. It's literally going to open your eyes to stuff that your past ego wouldn't let in. You are going to learn so much, Yes about Jesus, but more importantly how to build a relationship with him. An unbreakable, immeasurable and a never quitting bond that's going to stick with you for the rest of your life. You are going to learn so much about yourself that it's going to literally make you upset. It's not bad rage, but more like a "what the heck have I been doing my whole life up until this point," rage. There's going to be strategies learned to be a better Christian that's going to be ingrained into your heart like a tattoo. The feeling of learning and the feeling of growth is going to make you the most excited you've ever been in your life. This God is yours and this God will never leave you. He Exists, He is here.

"I exist to Humbly use my gift of connectivity to motivate, inspire and lead by example. Never ceasing to grow Gods Kingdom, with grace first, I surrender everything." That's your exist statement. The statement that Charlie will help you build and the statement you had memorized by that same days nightfall. You have a purpose bro. Without the School of Ministry you would've never learned why Zack Quilici exists on this planet. Yea you probably could've answered the "what are you good at?" question very broadly, but you knew this was for real, Jesus wanted more, he wanted your heart, your soul, he wanted to get to know YOU. You are going to realize that all these tests, your personality, your skill sets, your gifts are all to point to one thing. Your purpose and how you are going to use those gifts to grow Gods kingdom. This is going to be important. For the first time in your life, you cared.

You aren't going to believe some of the things you are going to be able to accomplish or get to take part in. From building amazing friendships to reading more books than in your entire life, to embracing others gifts and even taking a holy crap pill and going to Israel. The validation, the incredible reassurance that what you are doing and what you believe is the absolute truth. When you not only read or get taught something, but when you SEE it, touch it and smell it. Everything comes alive in the Bible. It's going to make that book a colored popup book. Your *heart before this was full, your faith was understood, and your soul was transformed, but this trip to Israel; It's going to change everything. There's no going back for you after this. You will say to God plenty of times throughout the trip and the upcoming years after it. "God, I am forever yours."*

If you learned anything from this past year Zack, it'll be the discovery of you. The real you, the one you've longed for your entire life. It makes sense now. You cannot be Zack without Jesus ever again. Without the School of Ministry, you wouldn't know why you exist. You will be so incredibly grateful for all the things you will learn from the most inspiring mentors. Just do something you've always had a hard time doing. Listen. Cheers to one more year of absolute greatness. Thanks Jesus.

So before the School of Ministry I had decided that I wanted a career in ministry and that ultimately I needed to do a lot of learning. So what I do? I just read everything and became a fan of reading. I know some of us struggle with reading, but I just want to give you one trick that helped me read more, especially in a busy lifestyle.

I like to call it the "car/truck book" and it's pretty simple. You put a book that you want to read in your car and every time you get in your car you read one page and before you get out of your car you read one page. Now stop and think about how many times throughout the day you get in and out of your vehicle? You can just imagine how many pages you could read in one day and you might get through a book in a week or even a month. But I can guarantee you if you stick to this plan semi-regularly you will read a book a year and that's better than most people .

Waking up to learning while developing a passion for reading is easily the greatest gift, because without learning and pursuing knowledge, life to me would be boring. I'm reading current books to get up to date in today's culture with Christianity but I primarily LOVE reading books from pastors or theologians who have passed away. I seriously never take the opportunity to actually read the thoughts, prayers and sermons from the best in the world for granted. We get the chance to walk alongside someone and do life with him/her and understand what made his/her brain tick. HOW COOL!

Do not forsake wisdom, and she will protect you, love her, and she will watch over you.
The beginning of wisdom is this: Get wisdom. Though it cost all you have, get understanding.
Proverbs 4:6-7 (NIV)

So I encourage you, like it says in Proverbs to seek and pursue wisdom to make sure that you are not getting complacent in learning. There is nothing worse than complacency, my friends. I've never heard someone complain about learning something new that they are passionate about. So whatever your passion is, go read a book about it and I guarantee it, you'll get excited. If you need a wake up call to apply, to write that book, learn that new skill, pursue whatever you desire in according to God's will, let me remind you that your life is very short. So just do it.

TRUST

13

TO PURPOSE

But you are the ones chosen by God, chosen for the high calling of priestly work, chosen to be a holy people, God's instruments to do his work and speak out for him, to tell others of the night-and-day difference he made for you—from nothing to something, from rejected to accepted.

-1 Peter 2:9-10 (MSG)

US AS HUMAN beings, Christian or not, all learn at some point that we are all made differently: different aspirations, different goals and different personalities. Again at some point in life, we discover what our "calling" is. Mostly materialistically driven, we needed to pick a career very early. We know now how plans change, but what doesn't change is the need for security: a good paying job, a nice house and of course, a retirement plan, a way to support yourself and maybe one day support a family. Blah blah, we all know what life's all about. Money. That's what society tells us is our purpose, to be successful enough to support a family and hopefully put away enough for retirement.

†

We all have a purpose, whether you believe in God or not. Being a Christian man , I believe that He has a plan, a design, and a blueprint for my life. He gives us gifts of all types, gifts that we need to use every day. We can't waste them. I understand that now, but I didn't before. Until the day I surrendered each ounce of my being to God is when I indeed discovered what my gifts were. Our gifts are powerful; we have the ability to direct traffic to save lives. Yeah, I said it, SAVE LIVES! Like a superhero!

> WE ALL HAVE A PURPOSE, WHETHER YOU BELIEVE IN GOD OR NOT.

(side note.. Can't finish this thought without first explaining my wish, if I could be any fictional superhero it would absolutely be a ninja turtle, the thought of eating pizza all day, still being able to have huge muscular quads and kick butt all day is a dream come true, plus I'm a dang turtle. I have yet to meet anybody that doesn't like the sea turtles in the movie Finding Nemo.)

We can just be completely obedient to God, and we can be advocates for Christ. How cool is that? From every walk of life, any situation, any diagnosis, any neighborhood, seriously, anyone from anywhere. You can direct them to Jesus who can ultimately save their life.

In all honesty, it's the way we were designed; it's how we were hardwired to live. God created and designed us to be a servant for his kingdom and use our gifts to build His church. These words might sting a little bit when you read this but it's the truth. Some of us have a "lack of feeling" God in our lives, and sometimes it's the lack of being a servant for Christ. You see our purpose and design was to serve and not to be a consumer. So many Christians show up to church to get a message to make them "feel good" and they have never volunteered a minute of their time. The feeling of "good" only comes from being the best servant for Christ that you can be and sometimes that can start with serving at your local church.

Some people ask me, "Zack, how did you find out what your spiritual gifts are?" Starting with prayer, asking those around me what I'm good at and reading what the Bible teaches about spiritual gifts. Check it out.

There are different kinds of gifts, but the same Spirit distributes them. There are different kinds of service, but the same Lord. There are different kinds of working, but in all of them and in everyone it is the same God at work

1 Corinthians 12:4-6 (NIV)

For by the grace given me I say to every one of you: Do not think of yourself more highly than you ought, but rather think of yourself with sober judgment, in accordance with the faith God has distributed to each of you. For just as each of us has one body with many members, and these members do not all have the same function, so in Christ we, though many, form one body, and each member belongs to all the others. We have different gifts, according to the grace given to each of us. If your gift is prophesying, then prophesy in accordance with your faith; if it is serving, then serve; if it is teaching, then teach; if it is to encourage, then give encouragement; if it is giving, then give generously; if it is to lead, do it diligently; if it is to show mercy, do it cheerfully.

-Romans 12:3-8 (NIV)

So Christ himself gave the apostles, the prophets, the evangelists, the pastors and teachers, to equip his people for works of service, so that the body of Christ may be built up until we all reach unity in the faith and in the

knowledge of the Son of God and become mature, attaining to the whole measure of the fullness of Christ.
   Ephesians 4:11-13(NIV)

I started with filling out an application to volunteer at my local church. It wasn't my time, but God's time. If I hadn't surrendered my time, I never would have figured out what my spiritual gifts are. It's like God designed a certain "flow" for us and we just have to hop in and let Him lead us with our gifts.

I think we can all agree that we were all born with a passion for something. It takes people a lifetime to find it or they find it right when they're able to make their own decisions. I think when people find what they're most passionate about, their real sense of purposiveness starts. But what if it was much more simple than that. So I decided to figure out every aspect and detail of what I'm passionate about through God's word. This verse makes it simple,

But seek first his kingdom and his righteousness, and all these things will be given to you as well   - Matthew 6:33 (NIV)

So together, let's stop trying to figure things out by ourselves, and as hard it is or how much it goes against everything in us, lets stop and open the Word of God and read what He says about our purpose in life.

He calls the unqualified. Noah was a drunk. Abraham was too old. Jacob was a liar. Leah was ugly. Joseph was abused. Moses was a stuttering criminal. Samson was promiscuous. Gideon was doubtful. Rahab was a prostitute. Jeremiah was depressed. David had an affair and committed murder. Elijah was mentally unbalanced and suicidal. Isaiah preached naked. When God called Jonah, Jonah ran away. Naomi was an old widow. Job went bankrupt. Peter betrayed Jesus. The disciples fell asleep. Martha was a worrier. The samaritan woman was a multiple divorcee. Zacchaeus was greedy. Paul was engrained in another religion. Timothy was too young and had ulcers. And Lazarus was dead..We are in good company.

- Toby Mac

IN

14

TO THE SEED

God has the tough end of the deal. What if instead of planting the seed you had to make the tree? That would keep you up late at night, trying to figure that one out.

-Jim Rohn

PULLING INTO the gas station I was thanking God I even had enough to get there. Moving to sunny Southern California was the best decision of my life but having a truck that has eight gas guzzling cylinders wasn't the smartest move on my part. Pulling in, I parked, and stepped outside to the beautiful and consistent 70° weather. Gas or not, having no snow was a blessing. I went inside and got in line to pay for gas. It seemed like I was handing over my whole savings account to the cashier. I had left my phone in my truck so I had nothing to use to occupy myself while I waited. I noticed that the cashier was a man dressed as a woman, with lipstick, nails and his hair all done.

As a Christ-follower, my reactions were minimal, knowing that he was made in the image of God. I instantly prayed for him. I did not care about the identity crisis this individual was going through. Unfortunately, I didn't say anything as I've learned to not say everything that comes to my brain. Did I want to say something that would plant a seed? Far be it from me to miss an opportunity to spread the gospel. I handed him my money and headed back to my truck to start pumping gas.

"Maybe he did know Jesus."

While I was beating myself up for not being able to say anything, a man came up to me and snarled,

"Isn't that disgusting?!"

He again asked

"Disgusting right?!"

I politely asked,

 "What?"

At this point, I noticed the man's eyes ripping into mine, like a bull ready to tackle a bullfighter's muleta. He wanted answers.

"Isn't that disgusting that they allow a man dressed as a woman to work there?!"

So that's what he was talking about. My mind raced,

 "How could you think of someone like that! They're made in the image of God! They're loved just as much as you are! How do you not see him in God's perspective?!"

I shrugged my shoulders and threw my hands up in the air like someone not understanding a foreign language. I mumbled back,

"Nothing we can do..."

I redirected my attention to the gas pump, trying to avoid the conversation. It worked. He just angrily got into his truck, slammed his door and yelled,

A couple deep breaths later, I was in my truck thinking, super confused about the whole situation.

I tried to wrap my whole head around the identity crisis that that man was going through and thought of the evil hearted man that was so insulted by the cashier. How do you get to the point of such anger over another human being's identity? What was his deal? What was the story behind the cashier's life? How insecure do you have to be to degrade another person's life just because of their gender? Why didn't I have the words to plant a small seed to the cashier? What could I have said to the angry man to let him know that Jesus loves him? All I knew is that Satan was written all over the situation.

†

The evil part of this story was that the man was degrading the cashier as if the cashier was the one with the evil and disillusioned heart. That cashier might have the biggest and most compassionate heart, but the man cursing at me about the worker obviously had an oblivious perception of what he was doing. The waking up needed to happen in both parties.

This was a heartbreaking situation that ended up leaving me with unreasonable and unrecognizable guilt. I sat paralyzed in my truck for about ten minutes. I wanted to go back into the store to do something, say something, stick up for him, SOMETHING. Nothing. I did nothing. I started up my truck, put it in drive and drove off. We could all have this perception of our actions. We can all bad mouth people, gossip, slander and disrespect human beings who were *also* made in the image of God without even knowing it. It's easy. Understanding how important it is to have a perception of *you* dialed in. Take a peek on what James has to say about words coming out of our mouths.

"A bit in the mouth of a horse controls the whole horse. A small rudder on a huge ship in the hands of a skilled captain sets a course in the face of the strongest winds. A word out of your mouth may seem of no account, but it can accomplish nearly anything—or destroy it!

It only takes a spark, remember, to set off a forest fire. A careless or wrongly placed word out of your mouth can do that. By our speech we can ruin the world, turn harmony to chaos, throw mud on a reputation, send the whole world up in smoke and go up in smoke with it, smoke right from the pit of hell.

This is scary: You can tame a tiger, but you can't tame a tongue—it's never been done. The tongue runs wild, a wanton killer. With our tongues we bless God our Father; with the same tongues we curse the very men and women He made in His image. Curses and blessings out of the same mouth!

My friends, this can't go on. A spring doesn't gush fresh water one day and brackish the next, does it? Apple trees don't bear strawberries, do they? Raspberry bushes don't bear apples, do they? You're not going to dip into a polluted mud hole and get a cup of clear, cool water, are you?

(James 5:5-12 MSG)

†

Now what about the cashier? There's not a whole lot to say about that man.. Do I desperately pray that I can have another opportunity to maybe plant a seed with him? Sure. I can also learn from this: never cease at an opportunity to spread the good news of Jesus Christ. Simply say to someone, *"Hey just want to say I'm hoping you're having a great day, I love you and so does Jesus Christ."* Guilt is a teacher because ten out of ten times there will be the feeling of *"Wow! I'm never going to do that again."* So next time, I'm ready. You need to do your best and be ready as well. No matter the situation, if the

Holy Spirit is tugging on you to plant a seed, don't miss it. Don't let guilt get a hold of you. Now I am going to give you an opportunity to read some of the Bible when Jesus talks about planting seeds in Mark four.

The Story of the Scattered Seed

He went back to teaching by the sea. A crowd built up to such a great size that he had to get into an offshore boat, using the boat as a pulpit as the people pushed to the water's edge. He taught by using stories, many stories.

"Listen. What do you make of this? A farmer planted seed. As he scattered the seed, some of it fell on the road and birds ate it. Some fell in the gravel; it sprouted quickly but didn't put down roots, so when the sun came up it withered just as quickly. Some fell in the weeds; as it came up, it was strangled among the weeds and nothing came of it. Some fell on good earth and came up with a flourish, producing a harvest exceeding his wildest dreams.

"Are you listening to this? Really listening?"

When they were off by themselves, those who were close to him, along with the Twelve, asked about the stories. He told them, "You've been given insight into God's kingdom—you know how it works. But to those who can't see it yet, everything comes in stories, creating readiness, nudging them toward receptive insight. These are people—

Whose eyes are open but don't see a thing,

Whose ears are open but don't understand a word,

Who avoid making an about-face and getting forgiven."

He continued, "Do you see how this story works? All my stories work this way.

"The farmer plants the Word. Some people are like the seed that falls on the hardened soil of the road. No sooner do they hear the Word than Satan snatches away what has been planted in them.

"And some are like the seed that lands in the gravel. When they first hear the Word, they respond with great enthusiasm. But there is such shallow soil of character that when the emotions wear off and some difficulty arrives, there is nothing to show for it.

"The seed cast in the weeds represents the ones who hear the kingdom news but are overwhelmed with worries about all the things they have to do and all the things they want to get. The stress strangles what they heard, and nothing comes of it.

"But the seed planted in the good earth represents those who hear the Word, embrace it, and produce a harvest beyond their wildest dreams."

Giving, Not Getting

Jesus went on: "Does anyone bring a lamp home and put it under a washtub or beneath the bed? Don't you put it up on a table or on the mantel? We're not keeping secrets, we're telling them; we're not hiding things, we're bringing them out into the open.

"Are you listening to this? Really listening?

"Listen carefully to what I am saying—and be wary of the shrewd advice that tells you how to get ahead in the world on your own. Giving, not getting, is the way. Generosity begets generosity. Stinginess impoverishes."

Never Without a Story

Then Jesus said, "God's kingdom is like seed thrown on a field by a man who then goes to bed and forgets about it. The seed sprouts and grows—he has no idea how it happens. The earth does it all without his help: first a green stem of grass, then a bud, then the ripened grain. When the grain is fully formed, he reaps   harvest time!

"How can we picture God's kingdom? What kind of story can we use? It's like a pine nut. When it lands on the ground it is quite small as seeds go, yet once it is planted it grows into a huge pine tree with thick branches. Eagles nest in it."

With many stories like these, he presented his message to them, fitting the stories to their experience and maturity.

He was never without a story when he spoke. When he was alone with his disciples, he went over everything, sorting out the tangles, untying the knots.

The Wind Ran Out of Breath

Late that day he said to them, "Let's go across to the other side." They took him in the boat as he was. Other boats came along. A huge storm came up. Waves poured into the boat, threatening to sink it. And Jesus was in the stern, head on a pillow, sleeping! They roused him, saying, "Teacher, is it nothing to you that we're going down?"

Awake now, he told the wind to pipe down and said to the sea, "Quiet! Settle down!" The wind ran out of breath; the sea became smooth as glass. Jesus reprimanded the disciples: "Why are you such cowards? Don't you have any faith at all?"

They were in absolute awe, staggered. "Who is this, anyway?" they asked. "Wind and sea at his beck and call!"

Mark 4 The Message (MSG)

†

This is where I'm going to be funny, if you send me a text (phone number in introduction) saying you read all of Mark four, I will send you a "good job" selfie picture and you can forever have a picture of my face on your phone.

HIM

15

TO THE LOVE

*God's love is so extravagant and so inexplicable that he
loved us before we were us. He loved us before we existed. He
knew many of us would reject him, hate him, curse him, and
rebel against him. Yet he chose to love us, God loves us because
he is love.*

-Judah Smith

*For God so loved the world that he gave his one and
only Son, that whoever believes in him shall not perish but have
eternal life.*

-John 3:16 (NIV)

I DON'T KNOW why this might be the only
vivid thing I remember as a child, but then again I do. It
still hurts and it hurts badly. I remember smashing my
back into this brick wall behind me, not knowing it was
there to catch me. Fully thinking I was going to the

ground, I thought, "Maybe this puddle of tears can catch me". But that brick wall is something I'll remember for the rest of my life. You see, my beautiful mother gave birth to my brother and I and it was the greatest blessing ever to have a co partner in crime in my life, but what was even better was having another set of twins as our best friends. Talk about chaos! The way we met was so amazing, as our dad was teaching us to ride our bikes on a beautiful spring day in Sparks, Nevada. There was another dad teaching his young ones how to ride the SAME EXACT BIKES! At that very moment we knew we'd become the best of friends, but our bike riding would ultimately lead to the biggest heartbreak of my fourth grade year. You see, the tears and that brick wall, was a part of not a bike crash that I was a part of, but a bike crash that led to one of the twins in the other family lives to be cut short. Leading me to the funeral home and tears were uncontrollable.

I remember not being able to see, not being able to breath; not being able to believe it was true. I just lost one of my best friends and this HAS to be a nightmare that I'm willing to wake up from at any dang moment now.

They couldn't stop the bleeding. They tried everything they could. I don't doubt for a minute that the doctors working on the little fourth grader weren't trying with all their might to save him. See, my friend had crashed pretty hard and so awkwardly on the ground that his main artery to his heart could not be closed unfortunately he bled to death. Ugh, it's bringing me back to the sad moment of our fourth grade class planting a tree for him and me having to scoop a pile of dirt into the hole. I didn't want to. I felt like this was it, once I threw this dirt it was a done deal. My friend was gone. My first true heartbreak.

Finding Christ just a few years ago made me rethink all my heartbreaks and what his love can really overcome. You see, in fourth grade, I thought I was going to die. In ninth grade I thought I was going to die. And three years ago I thought I was going to die. But now I can see the way God was with me through all of those. I have never and will never undermine how painful it is to get your heart broken into a million pieces by an event or someone you love. You don't know when it's going to end, it's all you can think about and you can't eat. Straight brokenness. But in all honesty, it might be the best thing that can ever happen to you. God can use broken people and it might not be until you're at your lowest point in your life that you decide you need God.

If it wasn't for the devastating heartbreak that I went through, regardless of the severity of it in comparison to other people's sufferings, I found Christ. That my friends, is the definition of love. It brings up a very recognized, albeit underused and underrated verse in the Bible. There is something that God did that ultimately let us know what true love is and where the definition of love comes from. I love looking at different translations of this verse,

> *"This is how much God loved the world: He gave his Son, his one and only Son. And this is why: so that no one need be destroyed; by believing in him, anyone can have a whole and lasting life. God didn't go to all the trouble of sending his Son merely to point an accusing finger, telling the world how bad it was. He came to help, to put the world right again. Anyone who trusts in him is acquitted; anyone who refuses to trust him has long since been under the death sentence without knowing it. And why? Because of that person's failure to believe in the one-of-a-kind Son of God when introduced to him.*

John 3:16-18 (MSG)

Reading that, understanding it to its core and making sure I believe it in my heart is what really healed me. And believe it or not, it makes me grateful for everything I have ever gone through: all the tears, depression, heartaches and anger. ALL WORTH IT. If you held out two hands and said I had a choice, one hand held the ability to have   ALL WORTH IT everyone or everyone that I have ever lost, back, or the other hand had held the love of Jesus Christ, I can easily say I'd choose Jesus over anything and anyone. Now I don't wish pain, anger or heartbreak on anyone, but wow, if that means in the middle of that hurt you found Christ, I'm ALL for it! Sometimes hitting rock bottom is the only way people can see the real love that God had for them from the beginning.

So thinking back at all the pain, I'm waking up to the fact that undoubtedly it was all worth it. Do yourself a favor. If you're going through something tough right now, or you've made it through something, as much as we might turn away from cliché Christian sayings like

"He's with you."
"Turn to God."
"Open your heart to God."
"God can heal broken hearts."

Cliché or not, it doesn't mean it's not true and if you've made it through something devastating, don't ever miss an opportunity, regardless if that person is in fourth grade, ninth grade or a grown adult. Hold their hands and pray with them. The real love of Christ might be on the other side of the pain, and from experience.

FOREVER

CONCLUSION

*"**I NEVER** FULLY grasped the phrase we are gambling on borrowed time". If we would really die at any moment, what impact would we leave? On March 31st, that was changed. Driving to church was a normal thing for me. I never feared that drive one bit until this lady decided to turn into me, sending me into a brick wall, causing me to ricochet back out over the sidewalk into traffic. My front two tires popped as well as all my airbags going off, my bumper and front was completely done. Three men pulled over, called 911, and helped me get out of the car since my door was jammed. I didn't get to thank*

them but man, I am thankful. The officer and paramedic said I was lucky that I wasn't more hurt or gone because of the damage. If I had hit that wall a slight bit more head on, I would be gone. I was in awe when I was sitting there awake and conscious. Adrenalin began to wear off, and the reality of what happened began to sink in. Tears began to fill my eyes from fear. My parents were called. All I wanted was to see my family at that moment but as all the eyes from other cars were looking at this accident, I couldn't help but think what their stories were. I had come to an "awe" standpoint of being gone in that very moment. God totally focused my mind onto the souls we have to reach. This accident was an awakening call to understanding how urgent we need to be with others' eternities on the line every single day. Every encounter should reflect the love of Jesus."

    -Avery Ringlever

      The perspective of life has to be shifted. It has to be urgent. We are talking about eternity here, and the truth is that we are gambling on borrowed time. That Our Heavenly Father can take us home at any moment. Just like my friend Avery said above, every encounter we have with strangers and especially with the people we love should reflect the love of Jesus, because there is no other way.

So my hope, gosh, I pray so much for people to have a mindset of openness, a mindset that won't be plugged or clogged with thoughts they are used to. Instead, have an ability to express interests of other thoughts, ideas, people and dreams to not get persuaded from the truth but towards it. Often we get so comfortable with the way our life is going and anytime someone has a different view on something, we get confused, we get uncomfortable and we shut down. Just because someone thinks differently, doesn't mean they are wrong, but what if they are right? Because the worst thing ever is to figure

I'D SAY LIFE DIDN'T START UNTIL I FOUND CHRIST

out that you've been missing out on the truth for however long. It often reminds me of the people that have been color blind for the longest time, who knows...decades. But there's this new technology out there where they themselves or family members buy them special glasses, that when put on, give them what they've been missing. They are able to see all the colors instantly and all the emotions come flooding in. They are hit in the chest with having a hard time breathing because the sky is so incredibly blue, they want to jump down on the ground in a push-up position to realize that, yes... the grass is really green. They even ask their family members what colors are what. Yes, they've grown up knowing that the sunset is a beautiful mix between red, orange and yellow, but they've never seen one. I'm somehow addicted to watching these videos on the internet. They are so special and so real that almost everyone can relate to them. This relates exactly how I felt when Christ opened my eyes and I started waking up to all the amazing and devastating things that this life really offered. I'd say life didn't start until I found Christ. It's overwhelming, but it's truly everything I wanted and everything I was designed for. To wake up and see myself and the world, just the way God wanted me to. Let's pray.

"God, thank You, thank You for allowing my stories to be used for this book, thank You for the reader of this book and thank you for sending Your son Jesus to die for us on that cross. I pray that myself and the reader who just finished reading this book will never stop pursuing You, never stop seeing Your goodness and never stop waking up to the life you have planned for us. I pray for continued humility. This book or anything in my life would not have happened if it wasn't for Your grace and mercy. My heart, my life and my plans are all Yours, forever for Your glory. Amen."

"This is how much God loved the world: He gave his Son, his one and only Son. And this is why: so that no one need be destroyed; by believing in him, anyone can have a whole and lasting life. God didn't go to all the trouble of sending his Son merely to point an accusing finger, telling the world how bad it was. He came to help, to put the world right again. Anyone who trusts in him is acquitted; anyone who refuses to trust him has long since been

under the death sentence without knowing it. And why? Because of that person's failure to believe in the one-of-a-kind Son of God when introduced to him.

John 3:16-18 The Message (MSG)

NOTES

1. David Bugenske, a radio presenter in Los Angeles, was at the Route 91 concert with his girlfriend. He's spent the month since the shooting meeting other survivors. http://www.bbc.com/news/world-us-canada-41792276

2. Chaper 8 page 155-157 "The Reason for my Hope" Billy Graham

3. Becoming a person of Influence Page 44-46 by John C. Maxwell

ABOUT THE AUTHOR

Gospel driven. Sanctification pursuing. Bible loving, smiling from ear to ear man. Author Zack Quilici wants to be known as someone who lives his life for Christ and nothing else. Residing in the beautiful San Diego region of San Marcos, California. He attends and works for North Coast Church.

Growing up in Reno, Nevada he is no stranger to activity. From football, basketball, snowboarding, golf, volleyball and Crossfit, you name the sport, he's there. He's been coaching fitness for almost 8 years and just loves when people get their first pull up!

Having his entire family in Reno makes it tough to be away, but he believes God has placed him right where he needs to be. With his mother Debbie, father Bubba, twin Brother Aaron, and sister Ashley cheering him on from nine hours away, it makes it easier to stay smiling.

His favorite things to write about are his experiences before God and how God had his hand in them the whole time. With the gift of transparency, you'll see his true heart and emotions in his writing.

His favorite place to write is at coffee shops, listening to acoustic alternative to get the heart and mind open. He is loud, genuine, people loving and would love to snag a cheeseburger with you after working out and then watching any sport anytime, anywhere.

CHECK OUT HIS LAST NOVEL "BE BRAVE"

Made in the USA
Coppell, TX
14 April 2020